WHO AM I TEACHING?

POPPY GIBSON

WHO AM I TEACHING?

How a better understanding of children improves primary teaching and learning

1 Oliver's Yard
55 City Road
London EC1Y 1SP

2455 Teller Road
Thousand Oaks
California 91320

Unit No 323-333, Third Floor, F-Block
International Trade Tower
Nehru Place, New Delhi – 110 019

8 Marina View Suite 43-053
Asia Square Tower 1
Singapore 018960

Editor: Amy Thornton
Senior project editor: Chris Marke
Cover design: Wendy Scott
Typeset by: C&M Digitals (P) Ltd, Chennai, India
Printed and bound by CPI Group (UK) Ltd,
Croydon, CR0 4YY

Library of Congress Control Number: 2024951377

British Library Cataloguing in Publication data

A catalogue record for this book is available from the British Library

ISBN 9781529684919
ISBN 9781529684902 (pbk)

CONTENTS

ACKNOWLEDGEMENTS

Thank you to the 35 contributors who shared their experiences and expertise within these pages and really helped bring learners' needs to life.

And thank you to you, the reader, for caring so much about your learners to want to read and know more that you have picked up this book. The best way we can continue to improve our teaching practice is through reflection, discussion and learning from others.

ABOUT THE AUTHOR

Dr Poppy Gibson is a Lecturer in Education at the Open University, England. After 11 years teaching and leading in primary schools around London, Poppy moved into higher education to work on primary education degrees, supporting students taking their steps to become primary school teachers. Poppy's research centres on wellbeing and mental health in education, and promoting positive outcomes for all our learners through inclusion and the fostering of safe spaces where students can thrive.

INTRODUCTION

WELCOME TO *WHO AM I TEACHING?*

We must begin with the opening question, 'who are the children you are teaching?' And, following this, how well do you truly know your class and understand their needs? The answer to this is probably as well as you can; you came into teaching to nurture, inspire and support vulnerable learners on their education journeys – not for money or fame (probably). But how much training and guidance have you truly had space for in one of the busiest, emotionally laden jobs, with your early starts and late finishes?

It is easy amid the termly chaos to lose sight of the importance of every single daily interaction that takes place between us and the learners in our class. Whether verbal or nonverbal, our behaviour matters, and their behaviours can help us gauge if their social, emotional and health needs are being met. After all, a behaviour is a child demonstrating a need that they wish to be met. But what may some of these needs be, and how can we meet them with consistency, compassion and kindness?

This book offers teachers a deep dive into some of the complexities that your pupils may bring into your classroom. Understanding the diverse nature of our schoolchildren here in the UK is essential if we are to fully engage and support our learners. This book enhances professional development, bringing a blend of child development, mental health and well-being issues, and practical day-to-day advice to new teachers to help better understand the primary school children in your class.

WHY IS THERE A NEED FOR IT NOW?

As the holder of this book, you may be in the best position to reflect upon why you have chosen to read this book right now. Are you a trainee teacher, learning and laying the foundations for your exciting teaching career that is yet to begin? Are you an early career teacher, developing your understanding as you make your important first steps in the education world? Are you an experienced teacher or leader, refreshing your knowledge and understanding of children's needs to best support your staff around you? Or perhaps you are in teacher education, helping raise the next generation of teachers, and wanting to ensure that you are modelling the essential skill of lifelong learning to your students. You may be in a role that isn't even listed here at all!

Regardless of your role, we can all agree that the dynamic between children and teachers is changing as we move forward into an age that is more information-driven and technologically aided than ever. The way we communicate is changing, too, and our relationships reflect our societal developments – hence why it is more important than ever that we reflect upon how best to understand and communicate with our learners.

This book is split into 13 chapters that aim to encompass a range of issues and needs that may be encountered in the modern primary school. Throughout these chapters you will also find thoughtful and reflective contributions from a wide range of educators, practitioners and parents to further embroider the topics under review.

Each chapter contains 'Reflective question' and 'Link to classroom practice' features to help you hone in on practical and purposeful tips.

As an experienced educator, I hope you will find this text informative, insightful and useful. I wish you all the best, and hope that you enjoy reading this book as much as I enjoyed writing it for you.

Poppy

Dr Poppy Gibson, Senior Lecturer in Education

1

CHILDHOOD IN THE 21ST CENTURY

INTRODUCTION

This first chapter reflects upon childhood through history and how children's experiences have changed over time, including the major integration of technology and the internet into society and our classrooms. It is vital that we as educators explore how the changes in the societal landscape influence the childhood experience of the learners in our classroom. This chapter is positioned before all of the others because, while we can appreciate that there are major political, economic and cultural shifts on a macro level for families, it is the nuances on a micro level that must also be acknowledged on a daily basis to help personalise meaningful learning. Bridget Halnan, Senior Lecturer, Specialist Community Public Health Nursing, offers a perspective on how health issues in childhood have changed over recent decades. This chapter also questions what the role of the modern teacher looks like in terms of being not just a teacher, but – among many other roles – a mentor, facilitator and coach. Primary school teacher Nick Huxley shares a thoughtful contribution on the way that technology and the integration of artificial intelligence (AI) is shaping contemporary childhood experiences.

CHANGING TIMES AND SHIFTING ENVIRONMENTS

We all understand that, from the Renaissance to the present, there have been considerable differences in the way Western societies have regarded childhood and treated children as a result (Cunningham, 2020). From being 'mini adults', to people that should be seen and not heard, social class and background have also played a huge part in how childhood has been experienced. Methods of upbringing, parental education, conceptions of parental roles and school provision have all changed over time (Shahar and Galai, 2023).

While we use the term 'childhood' to describe the age period we each pass through from birth to adulthood, the truth is that every single individual's experience of childhood is unique and personal, even between siblings or twins within the same family. No two experiences of childhood are the same due to a child's interpretation of these experiences, and the relationships held with people, places and things in their environment.

REFLECTIVE QUESTION 1.1

What was your childhood like?

You are most likely familiar with the concentric circles ecological model of Bronfenbrenner (1977) that shows the child at the centre of their own system, a system with five layers – starting in the middle with microsystem, then mesosystem, exosystem, macrosystem and chronosystem. Bronfenbrenner used this model to show how each level affects a child's development and growth, with those influences at the centre of the model being the most impactful on the child, and the understanding that the child's relationships within each circle subsequently affects their relationships in the next circle. Interestingly, in the decades following the creation of this seminal model, Bronfenbrenner shifted his focus from these environmental influences to development processes the child experiences over time in a *bioecological* model (Guy-Evans, 2024). Bronfenbrenner became more concerned with the proximal development processes, meaning the enduring and persistent forms of interaction in the immediate environment (ibid.). Bronfenbrenner also suggested that to understand the effect of these proximal processes on development, we have to focus on the person, context and developmental outcome, as these processes vary and affect people differently (Bronfenbrenner and Evans, 2000).

So, the takeaway from Bronfenbrenner's ecological theory is that:

> Teachers and parents should maintain good communication with each other and work together to benefit the child and strengthen the development of the ecological systems in educational practice.
>
> Teachers should also be understanding of the situations their student's families may be experiencing, including social and economic factors that are part of the various systems.
>
> If parents and teachers have a good relationship, this should positively shape the child's development.

> The child must be active in their learning, both academically and socially. They must collaborate with their peers and participate in meaningful learning experiences to enable positive development.
>
> (Guy-Evans, 2024)

LINK TO CLASSROOM PRACTICE: PERSONAL SYSTEMS

Give each pupil a page with concentric circles and a photograph of them stuck in the middle like the bullseye on a dartboard (or you could ask the child to draw themself in the middle).

Ask them to then write or draw (or use stick images or pre-prepared labels) into the circles considering how close they feel in certain relationships – such as a label saying 'grandparents', which they may choose to stick near the centre if they are close or may not even use that label if they don't have grandparents. This activity helps pupils to think about all of the different people and relationships in their life currently and the value of those connections.

In the first of two contributions in this chapter, Bridget Halnan considers how the landscape of children's health and happiness may have changed over recent decades, and why these might have changed.

CONTRIBUTION: CHILDHOOD HEALTH IN THE 21ST CENTURY

BY BRIDGET HALNAN – SENIOR LECTURER AT ANGLIA RUSKIN UNIVERSITY, A SPECIALIST COMMUNITY PUBLIC HEALTH NURSE AND FELLOW OF THE INSTITUTE OF HEALTH VISITING

The lives of 21st-century children living in the UK, according to the latest Millennium Cohort Study results (Joshi and Fitzsimons, 2016), are in many ways very different to their parents' childhoods. This study follows the lives of about 19,000 children born in the UK in 2000–02; it found in 2014 that their lives were largely enjoyable.

(Continued)

However, in the intervening decade, there appears to have been a decline in child health and happiness, including a fall in childhood vaccination rates resulting in a resurgence of serious disease such as measles (Wong, 2024) and an increase in rates of overweight and obese children. Over 20 per cent of five-year-olds are now overweight or obese, with a strong correlation between increased rates and living in poverty (RCPCH, 2023). Between 2019 and 2022 the number of children living in extreme poverty almost tripled (Bancroft and Mitchell, 2023). One in four children experience tooth decay, which is now the leading cause of hospital admissions in childhood – with the need for an anaesthetic, a procedure not without risk, for tooth extraction (PHE, 2020) School attendance for children who experience poor health will inevitability be affected. At the most extreme level, the rise in infant mortality rates means the UK is now ranked 30 out of 49 of the OECD countries, well behind other European countries, except for Bulgaria, Romania and Slovakia (OECD, 2024).

Post-pandemic demands on child mental health services have surged. In England alone, the proportion of five- to 15-year-olds with a mental health disorder rose from 9.7 per cent to 11.2 per cent in 2017 (NHS England Digital, 2018). Currently, the estimate is nearer 20 per cent for depression and anxiety (discussed further in Chapter 5), although an awareness of mental health problems has increased too, so longitudinal data need to be interrupted with care (NHS England Digital, 2023). However, research suggests that children with mental health issues have less favourable relationships with their peers, achieve lower grades at school and suffer more mental ill health problems in adolescence compared to children who had mental ill health problems 40 years ago (Sellers et al., 2019). There also appears to be a prediction of social problems at 11 in children identified with mental ill health problems at the age of seven. Regardless of whichever generation, mental ill health appears to be a predictor of lower academic achievement.

Good emotional health as a child appears to be the foundation for good life satisfaction in adulthood and although in the UK children and young people's happiness with their life is now at its lowest since 2010 a survey from Wales has indicated what children themselves really want to improve their health and wellbeing (Newton and Ponting, 2013). This research suggests they want:

1. more parks or green space, or for existing parks to be improved. Many UK parks are poorly maintained due to local authority budgetary constraints. While more generous funding may be available for larger parks, many children like to associate in smaller, local neighbourhood areas. These act as key places where they can meet up with their friends, play and be active;
2. a fifth of the children surveyed said they wanted sports facilities that they can walk to and are suitable for their age group. This ranged from wanting more specific sport clubs, such as basketball and football, to requests for more unstructured activity venues such as skate parks;
3. the survey went on to show 20 per cent of the responses wished for cleaner environments – particularly wanting litter and dog mess to be cleaned up – as well as requests for less pollution and more trees;
4. finally, nearly 10 per cent of responses were around road safety. This included requests for fewer cars on the road, speed limits, zebra crossings and more school crossing officers. The common theme appeared to be that children simply want safe spaces to play and be active. Data from the Royal Foundation and the London School of Economics has shown that the cost to society of not addressing these public health issues is more than £16 billion each year, nearly five times the total annual spend in England on early education (Centre for Early Childhood, 2021).

In conclusion, positive child health and the ability to access education are inextricably linked, but connecting data between the two has rarely been undertaken. One example of this link is Echild, a national resource linking together data from hospitals, schools and social care for 20 million children. Data shows the link between being born too early and adverse health and development. Chronic ill health, whether it be mental or physical, can result in school absences and thus underachievement at school, with the resultant impact on children's life chances (ADR UK, 2024).

TOXIC CHILDHOOD IN THE 21ST CENTURY

How often have you heard someone reflect that, when they were a child, they would have been out climbing trees or riding bikes instead of inside playing on screens? Maybe you yourself have said this.

REFLECTIVE QUESTION 1.2

Do you think childhood looks different now compared to how you experienced it and, if so, in what ways?

What things have stayed the same?

The current debate is the idea of 'toxic' childhood. Concerns in some literature warn that the modern world is 'damaging' our children, with at least 'one in five children in the developed world' diagnosed as having 'developmental or behavioural problems'; the number is rising by 25 per cent each year (Palmer, 2007). 'Toxicity' is therefore defined for this study as something harmful or detrimental to wellbeing, the latter being the ability to function properly and feel generally positive on a daily basis. In a thoughtful twist on this debate, Alexander (2007) argues that viewing contemporary childhood through a 'toxic' lens is unhelpful and can, in fact, be detrimental to children's learning. If children are 'obliged to begin from the premise that their culture – the building blocks from which their identities are created – is "toxic"' (Alexander, 2007: 57), they can become passive rather than active learners in their cultural world. Children learn to be cautious about dangers in their environment from birth, and if they end up fearing the introduction of new cultural tools, such as modern technology, they may avoid incorporating such tools into their lives. Avoiding cultural artefacts could reduce an individual's autonomy and thus hamper opportunities to learn and develop.

Alexander (2007) states that we should instead consider the 'vitality' of modern childhood, seeing the negative but also the potentially positive opportunities that living in the 21st century presents, such as globalisation and the integration of technology. To build upon Alexander's point, although the cultural artefacts and daily tools used by children during childhood may have changed, it is through the exploration of children's adoption of these cultural artefacts that we can better understand contemporary childhood. Through the lens of 'vitality' rather than 'toxicity', it is exciting to see how children can become active sculptors in identity construction and consolidation during childhood.

OUTSIDE TO ONLINE?

We may also consider that there has been a shift in the last generations from many children being mostly outdoors to largely online, or at least indoors with screens, despite research indicating that direct experiences of nature in childhood contribute to care for nature across the lifespan as well as supporting wellbeing through exercise, mindfulness and positive emotions (Chawla, 2020). It is worrying to see children become disconnected from nature, as this may lead to disconnection from caring about environmental issues, such as recycling and climate change. Equally, teaching children that their world is damaged and environmentally degrading can lead to ecoanxiety if they feel powerless to help prevent it (Chawla, 2020). Teachers now need to help children not only understand what is going on inside the classroom, but also outside it.

REFLECTIVE QUESTION 1.3

Do you think the role of the teacher has changed over time?

How does the current state of childhood need to be supported in our primary classrooms?

Research reveals a strengthening tension between the cognitive and emotional impact of screen use, raising the issue that our teacher training must more deeply cover understanding of technology as both an educational tool, that can have greatly positive outcomes for young people, and a tool of risk with addictive traits (Caballero-Julia et al., 2024). Teachers are well placed to help inform not just their learners, but also parents and carers about digital literacy and responsible use.

THE ROLE OF THE INTERNET AND DIGITAL TECHNOLOGY IN CHILDHOOD

Let us focus in from general screen time to the specific tool of the internet. Is connection to the internet enhancing or damaging childhood? Livingstone (2013) warns that the effects of childhood experiences are not yet fully understood, and thus we cannot even begin to assert or assess the risk or toxicity involved in children's use of online media. Livingstone muses:

> On the internet, we do not know how many children are hurt, or how severe are the consequences; there are no accident figures. If the offline were like the online, it would be like knowing, only, how many children report crossing a road and perhaps, how many report that something bad happened in consequence. On the other hand, if the online were like the offline, we would also know the online equivalent of how many cars were on the road and how fast they were driving (e.g. exactly what pornography they saw or how they were cyberbullied or groomed); most important, we would know whether an accident resulted (i.e. whether the child suffered harmful consequences, for how long and with what severity).
>
> (Livingstone, 2013: 18)

Perhaps part of the role of a modern teacher, therefore, is helping model and support children and young people to be prepared to navigate these new spaces.

LINK TO CLASSROOM PRACTICE: WHO INFLUENCES US THE MOST IN CHILDHOOD?

Try the Diamond nine activity.

You could ask your pupils to reflect upon the different influences in their life by providing each pair with a set of nine cards. Each card has something or someone shown on it that may influence a child as they grow: here are nine examples you could use: friends, parents or carers, nutrition, social media, grandparents, gender, wider family such as aunts and uncles, education, socio-economic status.

Ask the pairs (or groups) to order these into a diamond shape, with the most influential at the top of the diamond, then two on the second row, three in the middle row, two on the fourth row and one at the bottom that they regard as least influential. Figure 1.1 shows an example.

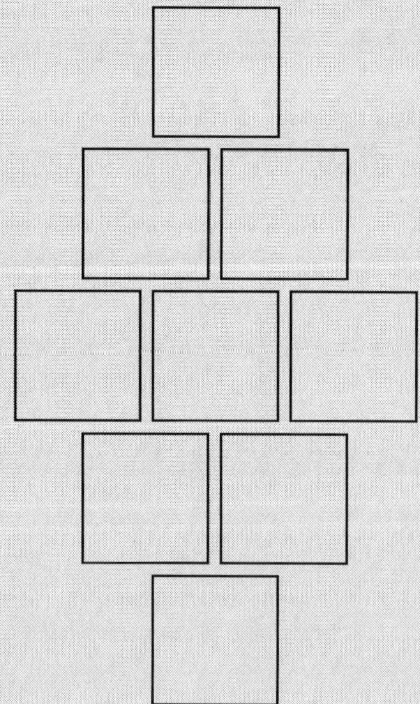

Figure 1.1 Diamond diagram

You can then ask around the room for each pair or group to feed back which card they put at the top of their diamond, and which card they put at the bottom. Did everyone choose the same or different? This sets a great foundation for a conversation on influences in childhood and development.

THE GROWING ROLE OF TECHNOLOGY IN CHILDHOOD, INCLUDING AI

Leading on from the previous discussion on technology and the internet, we end this chapter with a consideration of one of the most recent tools being developed in both education and society: AI. Are you an educator who is excited about AI, who is using it daily? Or are you hesitant about how AI might continue to change our world in unknown ways? This second chapter contribution from Nick Huxley considers the benefits of EdTech, including AI, but also the worries we need to consider as educators, especially when it comes to parental involvement and understanding.

CONTRIBUTION: EDTECH AS A TOOL FOR EMPOWERING PARENTS AND CHILDREN IN THE 21ST CENTURY

BY NICK HUXLEY, BSC (HONS), PGCE, MA IN EDUCATION – COMPUTING CURRICULUM LEAD AND PRIMARY SCHOOL TEACHER AT BALFOUR PRIMARY SCHOOL, BRIGHTON

In the rapidly evolving landscape of 21st-century education, the role of EdTech in empowering parents and children alike has become increasingly significant. As digital tools become an integral part to everyday life and learning – encompassing teacher, child and parental perspectives – they offer unprecedented opportunities to make education more transparent, collaborative and inclusive. However, these opportunities are not without challenges, particularly when bridging the digital literacy gap with parents. Drawing on findings from my MA research on parental involvement and digital literacy, I observed significant challenges that parents face in engaging with EdTech tools, which can affect their ability to support their children's education effectively.

(Continued)

At its core, EdTech has the potential to transform the traditional dynamics of education by bringing parents closer to their children's learning experiences. Online learning platforms, such as Google Classroom,™ allow parents real-time access to assignments, home learning (homework), grades and teacher feedback. This level of transparency enables parents to become more actively involved in their child's education, fostering a home environment that supports and reinforces classroom learning. From my research, I found that during the pandemic many parents appreciated online tools as they provided a direct window into their child's learning at school. While some parents highlighted the effectiveness of these platforms, others faced challenges, underscoring the importance of selecting the right tools to empower rather than deter parental involvement. Additionally, resources like instructional videos or virtual classes to observe lessons, as suggested by parents in my study, can further bridge gaps in their understanding of teaching techniques, enhancing collaboration between schools, parents and students. Moreover, communication platforms integrated into these systems make it easier for parents and teachers to share insights, address concerns promptly and work together to support the child's educational journey.

However, the promise of EdTech has not been universally realised. My MA research highlighted significant challenges in digital literacy among parents, which could impact their ability to support their children's education effectively. This digital literacy gap often creates a paradox where the very tools designed to empower parents can inadvertently exclude them. Without the necessary skills or access to technology, many parents struggle to engage with these platforms, leaving them disconnected from their child's educational journey.

The pandemic underscored these disparities in access to technological resources. As one participant in my research shared, 'remote learning required parental computer literacy … A barrier for those experiencing digital poverty', highlighting how socio-economic factors played a crucial role in shaping the home-schooling experience. Additionally, some parents expressed uncertainty and a strong dislike for using technology for home learning, with one noting, 'I have a hatred of Google Classroom! Fills me with dread!' These sentiments align with Ball's (2021) assertion of digital poverty as 'the socially uneven access to the internet and thus the inability to access remote learning resources' (p. 188), a challenge further compounded by feelings of uncertainty and apprehension towards digital platforms – an aspect of 'digital exclusion' (Ball, 2021).

These challenges are particularly pronounced in state schools, where outdated IT infrastructure and limited resources exacerbate the problem. During the COVID-19 pandemic, the sudden shift to online learning highlighted these disparities. Schools that had already embraced EdTech would have found the transition smoother than those with less technological infrastructure. Parents in the latter group who may have had limited experience with digital tools were often left behind, unable to support their children's learning effectively.

Despite these challenges, there are strategies to overcome these barriers and ensure that EdTech serves as a tool for empowerment rather than exclusion. One approach is a focus on building digital literacy among parents through targeted training sessions and accessible resources. Schools can play a pivotal role in this by offering workshops that introduce parents to the tools their children are using and providing ongoing support as they navigate these platforms. Additionally, simplifying the user interface of educational tools and providing content in multiple languages can make these technologies more accessible to a broader audience.

Furthermore, the introduction of AI in education is poised to revolutionise the learning environment for children, a shift that could significantly impact both students and their parents. According to a recent report from the UK Parliamentary Office of Science and Technology (POST) by Felix and Webb (2024), the effective implementation of AI in education necessitates evidence, training and clarity on legal frameworks, particularly to avoid exacerbating digital divides. The advancements of AI in education hold the promise of improving educational outcomes by providing tailored learning experiences and reducing the workload on teachers, allowing them to focus more on student engagement and less on administrative tasks.

However, the integration of AI in classrooms also raises questions about the role of parents in this new educational landscape. As AI-driven tools become more prevalent, parents may feel increasingly distanced from their child's learning journey, especially if they lack the digital literacy to engage with these technologies effectively. The digital literacy gap among parents highlighted in my MA research already hinders some parents' ability to support their children's education through existing EdTech platforms. The advent of AI could exacerbate this divide, creating a scenario where those who are unable to interact with AI-driven tools may struggle to stay involved in their child's education.

(Continued)

Furthermore, there is a growing concern about how parents perceive the use of AI in their children's education. While AI offers personalised learning opportunities, it may also provoke anxiety among parents about the potential for AI to replace human interaction in teaching, which is critical for developing soft skills and emotional intelligence in children. Felix and Webb (2024) highlight the need for ongoing dialogue between educators, parents and policy-makers to ensure that AI is implemented in a way that enhances, rather than detracts from, the educational experience.

Another critical aspect is fostering a culture of collaboration between schools, parents and EdTech companies. By involving parents in the development and refinement of digital tools, we can create solutions that are more user-friendly and tailored to the needs of diverse communities. By collaborating closely with parents, educators can ensure that EdTech tools not only empower families, but also effectively support student learning.

In conclusion, while EdTech holds immense potential to empower parents and students in the 21st century, realising this potential requires addressing the digital divide and ensuring that all parents, regardless of their background and digital literacy, can engage meaningfully with these tools. By focusing on digital literacy, simplifying technology and fostering collaboration, we can create an educational environment where EdTech truly enhances the learning experience for every child. Continued research is essential to understand how EdTech and AI can best serve diverse communities and ensure that every child benefits from these advancements.

LINK TO CLASSROOM PRACTICE: TECH REFLECTIONS

Ask each pupil to make a list of websites and apps that they use on any device. They could record this in a number of ways, such as a spider diagram with the word 'technology' in the middle, and then different websites and apps on each 'spider leg' coming off from the centre.

Then ask pupils to pair up and compare their spider diagrams or lists. Which apps or websites do they both use? Ask them to talk about why they use that website or app and how it makes them feel. What are the benefits of each of the apps they have listed? What are any possible negatives or risks of using each app?

SUMMARY

- Good emotional health as a child appears to be the foundation for good life satisfaction in adulthood.
- The common theme from research appears to be that children simply want safe spaces to play and be active.
- Teachers and parents should maintain good communication with each other and work together to benefit the child and strengthen the development of the ecological systems in educational practice.
- Teachers now need to help children not only understand what is going on inside the classroom, but also outside it in terms of supporting our environment and caring for our planet.
- The advancements of AI in education hold the promise of improving educational outcomes by providing tailored learning experiences and reducing the workload on teachers, allowing them to focus more on student engagement and less on administrative tasks.

2

CHILDREN AND THEIR COMMUNITIES

INTRODUCTION

This chapter considers identities in our learners, including the need for respect and celebration for all cultures and backgrounds. The part that economic disadvantage (or advantage) plays in achievement and attainment is discussed. This chapter also holds space for a discussion around bilingual, multilingual and English as an additional language (EAL) learners. In this chapter, we also share a thoughtful piece from Professor Jeannette Baxter, Research Lead for the School of Humanities and Social Sciences, on refugee education to inspire creative thinking around how we can welcome refugees into our school communities.

OUR IDENTITIES

Identity formation is a main adolescent psychosocial developmental task involving complex interconnections between different processes that are at the basis of one's identity (Negru-Subtirica et al., 2017). Adolescence is a particularly crucial time for identity development, as studies into ethnic and racial identity show (Wang et al., 2017); individuals are also developing the cognitive skills to understand these terms and their meanings. Staff working with children at primary school level are well placed to facilitate early conversations around identity and its many elements, such as:

- your values
- your personality

- your relationships
- your lived experiences
- your culture
- your ethnicity.

REFLECTIVE QUESTION 2.1

Often on application forms and surveys we are asked to tick a box to describe our culture, or background, or ethnicity.

What do you tick for these and how do you feel about these parts of your identity?

Getting to know the learners in our class is vital if we are truly to begin to understand their motivations and behaviours. This may sound like a giant feat when often we will only have one class for students for three terms, or less if you are a specialist teacher and may just see a class once a week, but there are simple strategies you can use to learn more about who you are teaching, and this will help nurture mutual respect between teacher and student.

LINK TO CLASSROOM PRACTICE: 'WHERE I'M FROM'

Give each child either a blank postcard, or a postcard template printed on paper (you can find free templates online). Ask them to illustrate the blank side of the postcard with either a place in their home town, or it might be several images of things they love about where they are from. On the other side of the postcard, they can write a fictitious postcard to the class saying things that can be visited, or eaten, or seen in their community. This activity helps individuals build pride in their community and share their favourite things about where they are from.

CULTURAL COMPETENCE

You may have heard of the term 'cultural competence' before; it refers to the ability to collaborate effectively with individuals from different cultures. Schools and classrooms are becoming increasingly diverse along a variety of dimensions, including migration; ethnic groups, national minorities and Indigenous peoples; gender; gender identity and sexual orientation; special education needs; and giftedness (Cerna et al., 2021).

We can see initiatives to support the celebration and respect for diversity such as the Fundamental British Values guidance produced by the Department for Education (DfE) in 2014. These values are: democracy, rule of law, respect and tolerance, individual liberty. Cultural competence can be developed by fostering inclusivity and diversity awareness within the classroom; the foundation of cultural competence lies in recognising and respecting the cultural backgrounds, experiences and identities of students, educators and communities (Eden et al., 2024a). By embracing cultural diversity and promoting inclusivity, educational institutions can cultivate environments where all students feel valued, respected and empowered to succeed (ibid.).

Amber Hadley, class teacher, offers this reflection on how cultural relationships play a key part in understanding communities:

> One aspect of attachment theory that I find particularly pertinent to education though is the contextual considerations, as in other cultures, emotional expressions that are coined 'normative' markedly differ because of human diversity (Keller, 2018). For instance, Western family relationships are especially dyadic, while in non-Western counties, relationships can be more polyadic, where infants participate in several proximal exchanges (ibid.). Due to these cross-cultural and cross-continental variations, attachment theory as it is comprehended by one society, cannot automatically be assumed to be comprehended in the same fashion by another society. I have learnt so far in my own education journey that when teachers appreciate that attachment can be understood differently across cultures, they are better equipped to communicate effectively with parents and caregivers from diverse backgrounds. I myself have witnessed how this understanding fosters stronger, more collaborative partnerships between home and school, which is essential for supporting students' learning and development.

LINK TO CLASSROOM PRACTICE: WHO I AM

Give each learner a piece of paper with an outline of a person on it or ask them to draw the outline themselves. Ask them to fill in the 'person' with things that make up their identity. It might be people in their family, or clubs they are part of, or a religion they follow. They can write or draw any things that help make up who they are. These people would make a great classroom display after being shared in talking partners; you could encourage the class to try and find peers who have drawn or written any same or similar things as them.

THE POSTCODE LOTTERY

The 'postcode lottery' is a term used to describe the significant differences in educational opportunities and social mobility that can be attributed to an individual's geographic location, specifically their postcode. This phenomenon is often linked to socio-economic class, with individuals from more affluent areas having access to better schools, resources and support systems.

Key factors contributing to the postcode lottery:

- *school funding*: schools in wealthier areas often receive more funding, allowing for better facilities, smaller class sizes and a wider range of extracurricular activities;
- *teacher quality*: schools in affluent areas may attract more experienced and qualified teachers, leading to improved educational outcomes;
- *parental involvement*: parents in wealthier communities may have more time and resources to support their children's education, such as volunteering at school or providing tutoring;
- *neighbourhood environment*: the safety, quality of housing and access to cultural and recreational opportunities in a neighbourhood can all impact a child's educational experiences.

The postcode lottery can have long-lasting consequences, influencing a child's future prospects for higher education, employment and social mobility. Efforts to address this inequality often involve policies such as targeted school funding, teacher training programmes and community-based initiatives to support disadvantaged students.

REFLECTIVE QUESTION 2.2

Reflecting back to 2020 when the COVID-19 pandemic caused school lockdowns in many parts of the world, which communities do you think were most affected and why?

DISADVANTAGED COMMUNITIES

COVID-19 lockdowns disproportionately affected disadvantaged communities. These communities often faced significant challenges, including:

- *economic hardship*: job losses, reduced income and increased expenses led to financial strain;

- *housing insecurity*: rent arrears and evictions became more prevalent due to economic difficulties;
- *limited access to resources*: lack of internet, technology and essential goods exacerbated existing inequalities;
- *health disparities*: pre-existing health conditions and limited access to healthcare made these communities more vulnerable to the virus;
- *educational disruption*: remote learning was challenging for students without adequate resources, leading to learning gaps;
- *mental health struggles*: isolation, stress and uncertainty contributed to increased mental health issues.

These factors further widened the gap between disadvantaged communities and those with more resources, highlighting the systemic inequalities that existed before the pandemic.

The postcode lottery also arises in the support for children with special educational needs and disabilities (SEND). Children with SEND will be discussed further in Chapter 9; however, the link here is to the disparity in how funding and interventions are designed and delivered depending on geographical location. In review of the 2014/15 policy of the Children and Families Act and Code of Practice, despite the policy's focus on children's needs, the current system is described as failing many children with SEND (House of Lords, 2022).

New research reveals that these children are significantly less likely to meet expected learning standards than their peers. This disadvantage is not evenly distributed; there is a stark postcode lottery in SEND education, with some areas providing significantly better support than others. This highlights the urgent need for reforms within the SEND system. The current policies are not achieving their intended goals and many children are being left behind. By addressing the systemic disparities and ensuring equitable access to support, we can help ensure that all children with SEND have the opportunity to reach their full potential (Azpitarte and Holt, 2023).

When we look higher at the provision for careers, we can see that the local authority provision for career support also varies according to postcode. Since the Coalition Government (2010–15), career support for young people in England has undergone significant changes. Funding cuts and a shift in responsibility from local authorities to schools have been criticised (Langley et al., 2014).

When funding and support is an issue, the one partnership we need to rely on is that between families and school settings; it is only when we communicate and collaborate that we can best support those in our care.

THE PARTNERSHIP BETWEEN FAMILIES AND SCHOOLS

The value of families and parental involvement in education can really make a difference (Lasater et al., 2023). Family engagement enhances classroom dynamics, improves teacher expectations and fosters stronger student–teacher relationships; it also helps promote cultural understanding, regardless of the student's age (Boberiene, 2013). Research suggests that family engagement can significantly impact children's cognitive and social-emotional skills, including motivation, attention and self-confidence (ibid.). However, changes in family structure have been linked to lower academic achievement (Heckman, 2008) through the family having different communication styles (Kelty and Wakabayashi, 2020).

When parents are involved, students tend to perform better academically, have better attendance and develop socially and emotionally. Community engagement extends beyond parental involvement, with communities providing resources, mentorship and experiential learning opportunities. These partnerships can bridge the gap between classroom learning and real-world application, fostering well-rounded individuals. By promoting inclusivity, diversity and mutual respect, these partnerships can create cohesive communities and address systemic challenges (Eden et al., 2024b).

ENGLISH AS AN ADDITIONAL LANGUAGE (EAL)

We will talk more about communication, including nonverbal communication, in Chapter 12; however, it fits within this chapter on communities in considering how children within their community may speak different languages to those used in the classroom. The acronym EAL is used to describe a diverse group of learners who speak English as an additional language; these children may be bilingual, speaking two languages, or multilingual, speaking several languages. Importantly, EAL is not a special educational need (SEN) and many children with EAL will be very able and highly academic; but sometimes the language barrier can delay full understanding and assessment of a child's abilities. Three groups of people who may move to a new country or community are as follows:

- *refugees* are people forced to flee their country because of war, persecution or violence; a refugee has a well-founded fear of persecution on the basis of their race, sexuality, religion, nationality, political opinion or membership of a particular social group;
- *asylum seekers* are people seeking protection from war, persecution or violence, but who have not yet had their refugee status evaluated by the authorities;
- *migrants* are people who choose to move to another country for other reasons (to be with family, for better job prospects, etc.).

But creating EAL resources goes beyond printing word bank worksheets and labels for cupboards; it needs to grow from empathy and compassion in the classroom.

SUPPORTING REFUGEES AND ASYLUM SEEKERS IN OUR SCHOOLS AND COMMUNITIES

In this section, we consider how we can offer safety and sanctuary for refugees and asylum seekers.

REFLECTIVE QUESTION 2.3

How can we support people moving from a different culture and country into our own?

What three things would be your priority to show or tell them?

SETTING THE SCENE: A DAY OF WELCOME

A Day of Welcome is a collaboration between UK Schools of Sanctuary and Anglia Ruskin University, led by Jake Rose-Brown and Jeannette Baxter. It is an annual day of solidarity and learning that aims to build a culture of welcome and understanding for people seeking sanctuary. By providing more than 60 free research-informed activities, teaching resources, training opportunities and live events, A Day of Welcome supports children and young people to understand the importance of building welcoming communities and helps schools to better educate and support refugee and sanctuary-seeking pupils and their families. A Day of Welcome is open to primary and secondary schools across the UK, and it takes place on the Friday before Refugee Week to maximise engagement in local and national activities.

The Day of Welcome's key aims are:

- to support schools to foster a culture of welcome, belonging and solidarity for those seeking sanctuary;
- to help teachers to uncover and share stories of refugee migration, local and global, past and present;
- to assist schools to better educate and support refugee pupils and their families.

CONTRIBUTION: A PATCHWORK OF STRANGERS: CRAFTING COMMUNITIES OF WELCOME FOR PEOPLE SEEKING SANCTUARY

BY PROFESSOR JEANNETTE BAXTER – RESEARCH LEAD FOR THE SCHOOL OF HUMANITIES AND SOCIAL SCIENCES, ANGLIA RUSKIN UNIVERSITY

What connects 16th-century refugees fleeing religious persecution from the lowlands of Europe, modern-day Norfolk school children and sanctuary-seekers from Syria? This short case study explores this question by narrowing in on the Norfolk delivery of A Day of Welcome.

We all have a role to play in fostering a culture of welcome and kindness and, as the centre of our communities, the potential impact of schools is huge. A Day of Welcome empowers teachers to unlock this potential by providing research-informed resources that are tailored to the contexts of various local areas and counties, from Norwich to Cardiff and beyond, which help school communities to understand how people seeking safety have played a part in making their own cities, towns and local communities the places they are today. Our work with schools to date shows us that involving refugee and sanctuary-seeking communities in A Day of Welcome activities and events strengthens links between refugee and host communities, and enhances understanding of sanctuary-seeking, both past and present.

Norfolk has a long history of welcoming people who have been forced to leave their homelands due to war, genocide and persecution. From the 'Strangers' of the 16th century, the Basque child refugees fleeing the Spanish Civil War and Jewish refugees seeking safety from Hitler's Europe to people fleeing 1970s Vietnam, the Congolese in the 1990s and more recent arrivals from Syria, Norfolk has always been a place of sanctuary.

As part of the 'Norfolk Welcomes' delivery of A Day of Welcome, school children aged between four and 18 years learnt about the rich and varied histories of sanctuary-seeking that have shaped, and continue to shape, the county of Norfolk. This included stories of how sanctuary-seekers, both past and present, have brought huge benefits to the county and its communities in the form of new skills, cultural and heritage practices, languages and food.

A key element of the Day of Welcome resources is creative response whereby pupils are asked to respond creatively or artistically to the refugee migration histories they have been learning about and discussing. Inspired by local stories of sanctuary-seeking, pupils from two Norwich 'schools of sanctuary' – Avenue Junior School and Hellesdon High School – created visual poems of 'Welcome' using a range of mixed media and textiles. This resulted in some very powerful messages of welcome.

(Continued)

Figure 2.1 'If you needed to run, I would be the sun to light your way': a mixed media message of welcome from a Year 5 pupil

Figure 2.2 'Refugees Welcome' and 'Welcome': hand-stitched messages of welcome by Year 9 pupils

FROM SYRIA TO NORWICH: STITCHING STORIES AND COMMUNITIES

Since the opening of the Syrian Vulnerable Persons scheme in 2017, more than 300 Syrian refugees have resettled in Norwich. As a City of Sanctuary with various 'sanctuary' groups and streams of action, Norwich has supported the Syrian families to integrate into life, work and school, and to take part in local sanctuary initiatives, including Norfolk Welcomes.

In collaboration with the school children from Avenue Junior and Hellesdon High and a Norwich-based refugee integration organisation, a small group of Syrian sanctuary-seekers took part in craft workshops in which they made colourful prints of their hands on fabric swatches. Two favourite colours chosen by the sanctuary-seekers were yellow and green, the colours of Norwich City Football Club, which is also known as the 'Canaries'. As it happens, the Canaries are named after the yellow birds that were brought to the city in the 1560s by the Strangers who were seeking sanctuary from religious persecution.

Figure 2.3 Green, yellow and black overlapping handprints belonging to recently settled Syrian refugees in Norwich

(Continued)

Over the course of a few weeks, the patches of welcome and solidarity were stitched together by a local sanctuary group called the Norfolk Knitters and Stitchers, who work closely with sanctuary-seekers in Norfolk and use their craft to support local refugee causes. The collective result was a 2m by 4m wall-hanging called *A Patchwork of Strangers: Norfolk Welcomes.*

Figure 2.4 *A Patchwork of Strangers: Norfolk Welcomes*

The wall-hanging was exhibited around Norwich to mark A Day of Welcome in Norfolk and Refugee Week before being divided into three panels and displayed in libraries across the county. It is a beautiful, and hopefully inspiring, illustration of how schools can work with each other and their local communities to create a culture of welcome and solidarity for people seeking sanctuary.

If you would like to find out more about A Day of Welcome and how to get involved, please contact Jeannette Baxter: Jeannette.Baxter@aru.ac.uk

LINK TO CLASSROOM PRACTICE: WHAT WOULD I TAKE?

Imagine if you suddenly had to leave your home and you only have space in your backpack for three items. What three items would you bring? When people have to flee their homes due to conflict or natural disasters, they often don't have time or ability to bring much with them at all; this activity can open up discussions on what it might feel like to be a refugee or have to leave your home and community, as well as building empathy and compassion to people who have to endure these moves.

SUMMARY

- The 'postcode lottery' is a term used to describe the significant differences in educational opportunities and social mobility that can be attributed to an individual's geographic location, specifically their postcode.
- This phenomenon is often linked to socio-economic class, with individuals from more affluent areas having access to better schools, resources and support systems.
- Family engagement enhances classroom dynamics and fosters positive student–teacher relationships.
- A multidimensional approach can promote equity, inclusion and wellbeing in education.
- Initiatives like the Fundamental British Values support diversity and inclusion in communities.

3

CHILDREN AND ATTACHMENT

INTRODUCTION

This chapter looks at a range of attachment theories and the links to emotional development and regulated behaviours. Ultimately, a child's attachments can have a significant impact not just on their education, but also through their journeys into adulthood. Five contributors share pieces on attachment to help stimulate your thinking in this area: Erin Skelton, Robert Archer, Lisa Gentle, Joanne Mullan and Amber Hadley.

UNDERSTANDING ATTACHMENT

Early attachment is essential for children. A suitable attachment with their primary carer helps form relationships later in life. If a child cannot establish a proper attachment, they may find it difficult to form any attachment with their practitioner. Having secure attachments and good role models helps children feel safe and secure, and more likely to be able to develop positive relationships in the future. There is, correspondingly, a relationship between poor attachment and depression; insecure attachment to primary caregivers is associated with the development of depression symptoms in children and young people (Spruit et al., 2020).

REFLECTIVE QUESTION 3.1

What do you understand by the term 'attachment' and why is it important when it comes to thinking about schools and education?

How can we foster healthy attachments in the classroom?

Making space to talk about things we are attached to gives insight to the child's home world and the relationships that they hold of importance. Role model by sharing insights to things in your world outside school, such as having a photograph of your pet on your desk that you can tell your class about, or sharing a memory of something from your childhood, or a holiday, to help show your learners that you are also part of a wider network.

LINK TO CLASSROOM PRACTICE: MY FAVOURITE CHILDHOOD TOY

Ask pupils to draw, paint or write about their favourite childhood toy. It might be one they still have or one they remember from the past. Ask them why it's special and how it makes them feel to remember it.

In the first contribution within this chapter, Joanne Mullan – the founder of Starra Education, which delivers accredited mental health qualifications – shares this insightful piece into different attachment styles and why we need to be aware of these connections.

CONTRIBUTION: SUPPORTING DIFFERENT ATTACHMENT STYLES

BY JOANNE MULLAN – PSYCHOLOGY TUTOR AT THE UNIVERSITY OF GLASGOW AND THE FOUNDER OF STARRA EDUCATION

> *The most precious gift we can offer anyone is our attention. When mindfulness embraces those we love, they will bloom like flowers.*
>
> Thich Nhat Hanh, 2017

Almost every teacher has a child who finds it challenging to pay attention in class, has trouble processing big emotions, or has difficulty forming relationships with their peers. Maybe you have noticed they are overly dependent on your approval, always seeking your attention, or quite the opposite – they keep to themselves, avoiding interaction with you or their classmates. While not unusual in developing children as they learn to

(Continued)

navigate school and its many demands, these behaviours might also be signs of insecure attachment.

But what exactly is attachment, and how do you support your students with insecure attachment styles? In simple terms, attachment is the emotional connection we form with others. While the most significant connections are those with a child's primary caregivers, children also attach to other significant adults like extended family and teachers.

Psychologist John Bowlby developed attachment theory to explore the deep emotional bonds between children and their caregivers. Bowlby studied the distress experienced by infants who had been separated from their parents. He proposed that early relationships with caregivers play a central role in a child's development. Bowlby believed that children come into the world with an inherent need to form attachments and that attachment behaviours such as crying were adaptive responses to separation from a primary attachment figure (Bowlby, 1982).

Children build secure connections when caregivers are loving, responsive and consistently meet their needs. They learn to trust caregivers and the world, become confident, learn to regulate their emotions and develop curiosity and eagerness to explore new environments, all of which are essential for learning and growth. Securely attached children are more likely to approach challenges with resilience and engage positively with peers and teachers.

Conversely, children who have encountered disruptions in attachments with their caregivers may experience feelings of insecurity and low self-esteem. This can have a negative impact on their ability to trust other people and effectively regulate their emotions, which in turn can affect behaviour and learning in the classroom.

Bowlby proposed that insecure attachment can take three main forms.

ANXIOUS-AMBIVALENT ATTACHMENT

Children with this attachment style are often anxious about the reliability and availability of their caregivers. This typically develops when caregivers are inconsistent – sometimes nurturing and attentive, other times neglectful or unavailable. In the classroom, these children are often overly dependent on the teacher for reassurance and show heightened anxiety if separated from their main teacher or when exposed to new tasks and situations.

AVOIDANT ATTACHMENT

Children with this attachment style learn to suppress their emotional expressions and may appear to be emotionally detached or indifferent to their caregiver. This typically develops when a caregiver has consistently rejected them or has been consistently emotionally unavailable. In the classroom, this might look like hyper-independence, rarely asking their teacher for help. They might struggle to form close relationships with other children due to the avoidance of emotional connection.

DISORGANISED ATTACHMENT

Children with this attachment style experience their caregivers as both a source of comfort and a source of fear, leading to a highly conflicted and confusing relationship. This typically develops when a caregiver displays frightening, erratic or abusive behaviour; this is often because of trauma that they have experienced. The child wants to be comforted by the caregiver but also feels scared of them. In the classroom, these children may have notable difficulty regulating emotions and display behaviours such as aggression and withdrawal.

A child's attachment style with their caregivers can influence their future academic success by shaping their motivation, attention and self-esteem. Secure attachment supports cognitive development, confidence and the willingness to explore, all of which contribute to better learning outcomes (Wang, 2021).

On the one hand, research shows that securely attached children outperform children with insecure attachment in mathematics, reading and linguistic skills, which may be traced back to the preschool age (Lyu, 2023). On the other hand, insecure attachment can lead to poor academic performance, communication and motivation (Moss and St-Laurent, 2001) and an increased risk of behavioural issues (Hutchings et al., 2023).

As teachers, our role often goes far beyond simply transferring knowledge. Understanding attachment styles is important if we want to support our students effectively, especially those who have experienced difficulties in their home lives.

Here are some guidelines you might find helpful when supporting students with insecure attachment:

(Continued)

- children thrive on routine and predictability because it helps them feel safe and secure; create a consistent routine in your classroom and stick to it as much as possible;
- show empathy and understanding; acknowledge your students' feelings and help them to verbalise their emotions;
- use positive reinforcement; be patient with disruptive behaviours, no matter how challenging this might be for you; remember that a child's insecurity may cause challenging behaviour in the classroom, so respond with understanding and care;
- celebrate your students' small achievements; this boosts confidence and self-esteem.

For some children, teachers may be the only consistent, caring presence in their lives. We can provide the stability and support that children with insecure attachments need. By understanding different attachment styles and how they affect our students, we can create a nurturing space where these children can feel secure, develop trust and thrive.

Note from author Joanne: My nan was my kinship carer, and we had the most beautiful times together. When I was ten, she died. My teacher, Mrs Marshall, wrapped me up in cotton wool. She was so kind to me, providing the warmth and security that a grieving child needed. The same attachment that my nan had always given me. I wanted to be just like Mrs Marshall and become a teacher who worked with children experiencing the kinds of things that I did. And so, I did. After a wonderful career as a primary teacher, I trained again in psychology and now get to teach attachment at university. None of this would have happened without Mrs Marshall.

LINK TO CLASSROOM PRACTICE: CREATE A KEEPSAKE JAR

Ask each child to bring in a jam jar or pot to decorate; supply coloured paper, stickers and beads for the class to decorate their 'keepsake jars'. Encourage them to keep it at home and put in special things to remind them of special times, such as a pinecone from an autumn trip to the park, or a feather they found in the playground.

In this second contribution, class teacher Amber Hadley considers how attachment in the very early stages of life can affect future outcomes.

CONTRIBUTION: THE RELEVANCE OF ATTACHMENT THEORY IN EDUCATION

BY AMBER HADLEY – PRIMARY CLASS TEACHER, WITH A PGCE FROM THE UNIVERSITY OF CAMBRIDGE

I would argue that attachment bonds during infancy and early childhood are absolutely vital to later outcomes in adolescence and adulthood – and that this is something for educators to be aware of. I proceed to explain why, using a combination of first person to reflect my own views, experiences and implications for myself as a practitioner, alongside third person, to briefly synthesise my research in this area.

Attachment theory can be ontologically understood as infants seeking contact with their caregivers, particularly when in a state of vulnerability or distress (Fearon and Roisman, 2017). Children begin to predict their caregiver's responses to this vulnerability or distress when they are just six months old (Benoit, 2004; see also Sroufe, 2005). Furthermore, an infant's attachment to their caregiver becomes increasingly selective at around seven to nine months old; they consequentially form a hierarchy of attachment figures around nine to 18 months old, where they recognise that their attachment to different caregivers varies (Zeanah et al., 2011; see also Benoit, 2004).

Attachment is an essential constituent of childhood, perhaps since infants have a biological disposition to want to form attachments with their adult caregivers, and they acquire such a strong, vivid – maybe even underestimated – understanding of whether or not they are accepted, loved and nurtured by their caregivers in the early years of life (Dykas and Cassidy, 2011). As a teacher, understanding this deep-rooted need can help in cultivating a nurturing classroom environment where students feel secure and valued.

Secure attachment is the most common type of attachment, which means that most infants and children feel safe, comforted and protected, thus fostering mutually positive, trusting relationships (Ali et al., 2021). But, comparatively,

(Continued)

the second most common type of attachment is what is known as *insecure avoidance*, where children (at times even infants) present as hostile towards others, deriving from a masking of negative, traumatising emotions – notably the overwhelming feeling of being rejected by the caregiver (Mercer, 2011). Yet, because attachment styles are so dynamic, it is most beneficial to avoid a reductionist approach. For these reasons, rather than focusing on attachment as a construct itself, research exponentially explores attachment quality through analyses of seminal, contemporary and longitudinal studies (Benoit, 2004; see also Fearon and Roisman, 2017).

Additionally, the historical paradigm proposed for decades was that because mothers were the primary caregivers in nuclear families, infants would only form attachments to their mothers, but there are plenty of works that counteract this, purporting that infants form attachments with multiple caregivers including their fathers, adoptive parents and foster parents, although this is not exhaustive (Ranson and Urichuk, 2008). Again, this is important for teachers and other educational professionals, as understanding this equates to a better understanding of the family dynamics of their students. Moreover, I propose that acknowledging children are products of multiple influences, of nature and of nurture, increases our sensitivity to the emotional needs of the children we teach, encouraging educators to deploy a holistic approach to their practice, ergo allowing teachers to tailor their classroom strategies accordingly.

Finally, outcomes are described as more austere for those who are *insecure avoidant* in the Early Years, and insecure individuals often suppress social information pertaining to their attachment experiences later in childhood (Dykas and Cassidy, 2011). They commonly avoid encoding emotional and physical memories; hence they are often guarded and aloof compared to individuals with a secure attachment style, who temporarily tolerate their distress rather than deny its existence (ibid.).

It is my belief that teachers who understand this attachment style can better interpret these behaviours not as signs of disengagement or defiance, but as coping mechanisms and innate responses to tenuous relationships with caregivers. In my view, all behaviour is communication, conveying a message to teachers, however overtly or covertly. Recognising this allows educators to respond with empathy and appropriate support, rather than with punitive measures, which could further alienate the child.

Lacking attachment, and not having needs met in early childhood, can lead to children having to meet their own needs through whatever ways they can find. Children who have not been helped to coregulate with a parent or carer have to find their own way to regulate over time. Parent–child attachment is a key dimension of the early emotional socialisation environment, and in subsequent development of skills in regulation when we feel frustrated or angry (Boldt et al., 2020).

REFLECTIVE QUESTION 3.2

In what ways can you help self-regulate if you find yourself feeling stressed or overwhelmed?

SECURE BASE SCRIPT

Have you heard of the *secure base* concept? In the following contribution from Dr Lisa Gentle, this concept is explained and the links to education are highlighted.

CONTRIBUTION: THE RELEVANCE OF THE SECURE BASE SCRIPT CONCEPT TO SCHOOL STAFF

BY DR LISA GENTLE – RESEARCH FELLOW AND RESEARCH MANAGER AT NORLAND COLLEGE

The secure base concept is central to attachment theory and yet its relevance to educator–pupil relationships is often overlooked (Waters and Cummings, 2000; Parr, 2019). A secure base is someone who acts as a safe haven for a child which results in them developing the confidence to explore from the base, because they are certain that when they return they will be welcomed, emotionally and physically nourished, comforted and reassured if they are distressed or frightened, and that the secure base will only intervene or guide them when necessary (Bowlby, 1988).

The core elements of effective secure base interactions at times when help is needed are represented in a list called the *secure base script* (Waters and

(Continued)

Waters, 2006). Adults acting as an effective secure base and children using a secure base efficiently take the following approach to support-seeking and support-providing interactions:

- the adult and child are constructively occupied (together or independently);
- an event or person causes the child distress;
- the child makes a bid for help;
- the bid for help is detected by the secure base and they offer help;
- the child accepts the offer of help;
- the help is appropriate and effective in overcoming the difficulty;
- the help includes effective comforting and leads to affect regulation (the emotional state and mood calm);
- the adult and child return to constructive engagement.

A person's past experiences of secure base interactions shape their unconscious knowledge of the script, which subsequently informs their secure base behaviours (Huth-Bocks et al., 2022). Some staff therefore instinctively provide pupils with a secure base, and pupils who have had secure experiences are likely to already be effective at using a secure base for support. However, other staff and pupils will have had experiences leading to assumptions that make it difficult for them to use or be a secure base – in which case, either one may inadvertently disrupt the process.

Importantly, a person's unconscious secure base script knowledge also influences the way they believe they should mentor others facing education-related challenges (Gentle, 2024). While the script sounds logical, and many believe they adhere to it, we all know people who are unable to ask for help, ignore bids for help, offer inappropriate help, have difficulty accepting help, or find it difficult to achieve affect regulation when they receive help. Fortunately, a person's script knowledge is revised and updated across their lifespan in response to new experiences and if they develop their understanding of situations and approaches (Andriopoulou, 2022).

When school staff act as a secure base for pupils alongside addressing their individual needs it increases the likelihood of pupils developing the confidence to ask them for assistance, guidance and reassurance when necessary, which enables successful problem resolution and affect regulation, which then allows pupils to direct their attention to exploration, experimentation and learning (Parker and Rose, 2014; Williford et al., 2016; Parr, 2019). In contrast, when pupils' bids for help are misunderstood or disregarded it disrupts the process leading to resolution and affect regulation and means constructive engagement in the form of exploration or learning cannot resume unless pupils are willing to do so without the comfort of knowing there is reliable and trustworthy support if they encounter a difficulty (Gilbert et al., 2021; Currigan and Shackleton, 2022). Therefore, pupils' healthy dependence on staff who act as secure bases supports the development of their independence and confidence to explore and learn (Bretherton, 1985).

Understanding the secure base script and using it to guide interactions during times of difficulty has potential to improve staff awareness of the extent to which they notice, respond to and address pupils' bids for help, and how effective they are at seeking and responding to help from colleagues during their own times of need (Gentle, 2024). This will benefit pupils who will be able to use self-aware staff as a secure base from which to explore and learn.

OUR ROLES AS EDUCATORS IN ATTACHMENT

If we reflect upon what encouraged us to become teachers, or teaching assistants, there are many reasons that may have driven us. However, for many of us the core vision will likely have centred around wanting to support children and young people in their development and growth. As we have highlighted through this chapter, lack of attachment can stunt emotional growth which in turn can hinder learning. In this next contribution, Dr Robert Archer shares a personal reflection on how understanding attachment improved his practice.

CONTRIBUTION: CHILDREN AND ATTACHMENT

BY DR ROBERT ARCHER – INDEPENDENT RESEARCHER

The attachment system, shaped by the internal working model, influences our behaviour throughout life, particularly in moments of threat, stress, or fatigue (Riley, 2011). This insight helps us understand why children form

(Continued)

different kinds of relationships and why some of these can be more challenging than others. Had I been aware of attachment theory before I began teaching a Year 4 class in 2003 – especially how early emotional development profoundly affects children's ability to engage in positive social interactions and effective learning – I might have been better prepared to manage the confusing, negative and sometimes toxic behaviours I encountered. Additionally, I could have planned lessons that were more attuned to my pupils' differing attachment styles.

However, my teaching assistant and I worked together to create a safe, warm and welcoming environment with clear and consistent routines. We endeavoured to focus on building and maintaining responsible, reciprocal positive relationships rather than simply 'managing' the children in our care (Howes and Ritchie, 2002). Drawing from this experience, my advice to anyone new to teaching is that working with young children who display varying degrees of insecure attachment requires considerable time, emotional energy and sustained commitment to create a secure base. Although it took four months for all our Year 4 children to feel secure enough to trust us, the role we played in helping children overcome their insecurities and improve academically gave us a deep sense of personal accomplishment and fulfilment.

Finally, while understanding attachment theory might have improved my teaching practice, I acknowledge that I would have been uncomfortable examining my unconscious patterns of responding to confrontational and negative behaviour. It was only after transitioning to secondary teaching that I became more open to exploring these unconscious ways of relating to students and colleagues. This openness helped me better understand – and navigate – challenging behaviour.

In this regard, the psychoanalytic concept of projective identification was particularly helpful (see Curtis, 2015, for a very accessible introduction to psychoanalytic concepts). Projective identification involves unconsciously projecting unmanageable or unwanted emotions onto another person, who may then unconsciously internalise and act out these emotions. Individuals with insecure attachment styles are more likely to engage in this process, as they struggle to regulate their emotions. Consequently, attachment-insecure children may unconsciously project their anxiety, anger, or insecurity onto others, particularly teachers, as a way of coping with overwhelming emotions.

However, by understanding projective identification and its role in the behaviour of attachment-insecure children, staff can avoid becoming entangled in these projected emotions. This understanding allows for a calm response, crucial for effectively handling challenging behaviour and maintaining a safe environment.

LINK TO CLASSROOM PRACTICE: DESERT ISLAND TRIP

Ask the class who they would each take with them to a desert island and why? It is because of their certain skills? Or their personality? Or what other reasons? Remember to role model by also sharing who you would take with you and why.

HOW MIGHT POOR ATTACHMENT MANIFEST IN BEHAVIOUR?

In the final section of this chapter, we consider how poor attachment may manifest in the classroom. We have already mentioned how not having strong attachment with a primary caregiver in early childhood may affect a child's ability to self-regulate when frustrated or angry, so there may be issues around regulation and keeping calm, especially in social situations or times of difficulty with academic work.

CONTRIBUTION: 'WHAT CAN I DO TO SUPPORT YOU?'

BY ERIN SKELTON – CHIEF STRATEGY OFFICER AT BRIGHT FIELD CONSULTING AND A TEACHER OF PSYCHOLOGY, CRIMINOLOGY AND RELIGIOUS STUDIES AT WORKSOP COLLEGE

Every September begins in exactly the same way for me: looking at class lists, SIMs or iSAMS data, cross-referencing that with CPOMS, school records and class photos and then using my teacher intuition to answer the two most

(Continued)

important questions I will ask my students all year: 'Who are you?' and 'What can I do to support you?'

I have always been very aware of the impact of attachment styles on how we approach building positive teacher–student relationships, how certain attachment styles show up in different ways and how students can have a combination of styles because attachment occurs over time (Bergin and Bergin 2009). I appreciate the challenge for teachers in trying to truly understand the internal and external factors that produce the behaviours and challenges our students face.

Some of our 'perfect' students, who are so often described as independent high-achievers and who can be perceived by their teachers as driven and sometimes lacking in warmth, can hide avoidant attachment styles. Learning that total self-sufficiency is their best coping mechanism, these students might struggle with group work, not be able to use creative problem-solving or be imaginative, and struggle to build trust with adults. They will constantly ask if they have written enough, tear out pages from their exercise books if it isn't perfect and, in the age of AI, will often be caught out by leaning too heavily on it to find answers. They often have exceptional attendance records.

Some of our 'attention-seeking' students who are overly talkative, shout out and distract their peers can hide ambivalent attachment styles. They mask a hyper-awareness of adult behaviour, anxiety about not having their needs met and often believe that relationships are transactional, so they have to do something to gain adult attention. They can present as underachieving or as perfectionists; they often struggle to accept support but will be unable to complete tasks; and their fear of building rapport with their teacher will often be channelled into disliking a topic or hating a subject. They can take instructions verbatim and struggle in learning where there isn't a clear answer because they fear the consequences.

Often our students who struggle to regulate their emotions and who don't cope with traditional behaviour management techniques are those who have disorganised attachment styles. They struggle with attendance and are more likely to truant or hide when they are in crisis. They frequently present as underachieving and will struggle to begin tasks because their belief in their own abilities or self-worth is so low. They also often struggle with a lack of structure or without clear communication of expectations.

As a teacher and educational consultant, I have always believed that building positive relationships with students that acknowledges their possible attachment style is crucial. But how do you do this? I am not an educational psychologist, but I am a teacher and a senior leader with experience across a wide range of educational settings. I am also an adult with a high ACE (adverse childhood experiences) score who personally understands the positive impact teachers can have in the lives of the students they teach.

My practice inside classrooms and school corridors has always been to build relationships in layers. It starts with learning everyone's name, correct pronunciation and to triangulate the information I have access to about them. I have a book of all of the printouts of their photos and go over them until I can remember every student that I'm likely to come into contact with by sight.

I am curious about all of my students and start every class in September every year the same way – we do an all about me exercise that focuses on likes and dislikes, I ask if there is anything they want to share with me and anything they think I need to know that will help them. I prepare mine in advance and I model authenticity and vulnerability in that activity. I share favourite food, video games, TV, music, etc. From day one, I am honest, humorous and caring.

My classroom is a safe space academically. We start the year off with erasable pens. I do academically challenging tasks but with low-risk outputs and give my classes lots of choice about how they undertake their work. We have rote phrases like 'there's no such thing as a stupid question', 'what is the worst that could happen?' and 'you've got this'. I also have a flexible approach to behaviour which is consistent in how it addresses the needs of my students individually and is not one-size-fits-all. I reward effort, academic risk-taking and vulnerability and not output or performance; I scaffold written work to ensure that there are no limits to the possibilities in my classroom. I teach them that cogent and clear answers are more valuable than lengthy, verbose ones and that creativity, problem-solving and emotional intelligence (EQ) are infinitely valuable.

Over time my students accept that I care about them because I am consistent in my approach outside the classroom. I go out of my way to say hello to them, make sure that they see me out and about at break and lunch, and

(Continued)

go to as many extra-curricular events as I can. I make a point of popping into lessons in my PPA to see their work and to praise them in classrooms that aren't my own. I really get to know them and in doing so I become a non-threatening, consistent, adult role model, who is relatable and kind and who approaches pastoral and academic issues with supportive solutions.

To get the best out of a pupil, you have to really know them, be invested, curious and caring. With students with high ACE scores, childhood trauma or complex attachment styles, it's about making them feel valued, respected and cared for in your classroom and beyond. It is not an easy journey as these students have complex lives and relational styles, but it is vastly rewarding.

SUMMARY

- Attachment theory can be ontologically understood as infants seeking contact with their caregivers, particularly when in a state of vulnerability or distress.
- A child's attachment style with their caregivers can influence their future academic success by shaping their motivation, attention, and self-esteem.
- Secure attachment supports cognitive development, confidence and the willingness to explore, all of which contribute to better learning outcomes.
- Attachment theory offers educators invaluable insights into the foundational relationships that shape a child's emotional and social development.
- Understanding and appreciating attachment allows teachers and other educational professionals to approach each child with empathy, recognising that behaviours often reflect deeper emotional experiences.

4

TRAUMA, GRIEF AND LOSS

INTRODUCTION

This chapter looks at how adverse childhood experiences (ACEs), trauma, grief and loss can affect a child and their behaviour in the classroom. The importance of caring sensitively for children who have been in the care system, fostered or adopted is discussed. The concept of 'death' and bereavement for children is explored, along with suggestions on how to facilitate gentle conversations in the classroom about grief. Interwoven with three thoughtful contributions from experienced practitioners, this chapter shares sensitive and purposeful strategies and activities to employ in the classroom to support children with trauma, loss and grief.

WHY UNDERSTANDING ATTACHMENT AND TRAUMA IS SO IMPORTANT

In Chapter 3 we looked at attachment and different attachment styles and reflected on why it is so important to consider a child's network and relationships when developing an educational relationship with them in the classroom. Where many schools are working to a busy curriculum, and with a strong accountability for assessments, often the children's backgrounds and needs seem secondary to the need to meet learning objectives; but how can children fully focus on a mathematics lesson, for example, when they are worried who might be coming through the classroom door next?

Children need to learn resilience as early as possible. Stability means an individual knows how to bounce back from adversity more quickly. Resilient children have the confidence to reason and can rely on their support network to overcome problems. There must also be consideration of how we use the word 'resilience' in schools, where we talk about children's ability for reframing resilience as overcoming vulnerability. Understanding a child's need to feel safe in their environment is fundamental before any bigger courageous steps can be taken.

ADVERSE CHILDHOOD EXPERIENCES (ACES)

It is essential that educators and caregivers understand what ACEs are and how they may affect those children as they grow and develop into adults.

REFLECTIVE QUESTION 4.1

How do you understand the term 'adverse childhood experiences'?

What events may fall under this umbrella; do you regard yourself as having survived any ACEs?

Below is a list of definitions according to the ACE definitions CDC-Kaiser ACE Study (Felitti et al., 1998), within the three categories of *abuse*, *household challenges* and *neglect*:

- *abuse*
  - emotional abuse
  - physical abuse
  - sexual abuse
- *household challenges*
  - mother treated violently
  - household substance abuse
  - mental illness in household
  - parental separation or divorce
  - criminal household member
- *neglect*
  - emotional neglect
  - physical neglect.

ACEs can affect holistic development negatively; individuals with ACEs are more prone to developing mental and physical health problems later in life. Many individuals may develop drug and alcohol problems in adulthood as a coping mechanism to process difficult memories and experiences and, the more ACEs that a person has, the more likely they are to develop mental illnesses such as anxiety, depression and other more severe conditions such as psychosis.

The link between mental health and physical health is apparent when we explore the literature on individuals who have experienced four or more ACEs, well documented since the original CDC-Kaiser study in the late 1990s (Boullier and Blair, 2018). Those people who have experienced four or more ACEs are at significantly increased risk of chronic disease such as cancer, heart disease and diabetes as well as mental illness and health risk behaviours (ibid.).

SAFEGUARDING

Trauma can impact a child's education. Those working with children must receive regular training in safeguarding to remain updated with workplace safeguarding and protection policies, as well as safeguarding officers' names and telephone numbers. Early alerts can prevent children from suffering abuse and consequences for longer than necessary. Having legislation and safeguarding policies in place and being aware of the government Prevent strategy will provide safer environments for children. Abuse and harm come in many forms, and the Prevent strategy, introduced in 2003 by the New Labour government fronted by Tony Blair, was introduced to protect individuals from extremism and possible radicalisation by raising awareness of signs and symptoms of abuse and grooming in children and vulnerable people.

Emotional neglect can lead to poor school attendance causing poor academic achievement and impacting their ability to reach their potential or get a job. ACEs can cause toxic stress, impacting the brain and affecting how the body responds to stress, but preventing early trauma can improve adult mental health. Research shows that children and young people who experience adverse childhood trauma are more likely to engage in early sexual activity and have a teenage pregnancy. They are also more likely to be sexually abused, exploited and forced to do things they feel uncomfortable doing.

The first contribution in this chapter comes from David Mather – a thoughtful reflection on the need for a strong partnership approach between schools, families and wider agencies to best support the children in our care.

CONTRIBUTION: TRAUMA, GRIEF AND LOSS IN THE PRIMARY EDUCATION CONTEXT

BY DAVID MATHER – SENIOR LECTURER IN EDUCATIONAL LEADERSHIP AND MANAGEMENT, AT THE UNIVERSITY OF PORTSMOUTH

Understanding trauma, grief and loss is crucial in the primary education context, where children face various challenges that can impact their emotional and psychological wellbeing. These experiences are not limited to any specific group; all primary school children may face trauma, grief and loss in different forms. As such, a nuanced understanding and supportive framework are essential for the foundations of a school community in order to help all children navigate these difficult experiences. Finding mutual understanding of what trauma means is essential, as definitions can be uniquely personal among those concerned.

Attachment theory has been shared widely and provides a foundation for understanding the emotional bonds that children form with those who care for them. If accepted in the spirit that is intended, we can acknowledge that stability is significant in a child's emotional development – for example, when considering the lives of children from service families, where a parent is in the armed forces; these children often face unique attachment challenges due to frequent relocations and parental deployments. However, these instances are equally relevant to children experiencing instability or separation in other contexts. In supporting children, the school community must recognise the significance of these bonds – meaning that structures should exist to maintain consistency and support in the classroom to the greatest extent possible.

Implementing a trauma-informed curriculum involves recognising the pervasive impact of trauma and creating a learning environment that promotes safety, trust and empowerment. For example, incorporating flexible seating arrangements, quiet spaces and embedded routines can help children with their feelings of security. These principles can be broadly applied, ensuring that all children benefit from a stable school environment. Classroom adjustments that benefit children experiencing trauma can be highly effective. One practical example is the use of visual schedules and clear, consistent modes of communication. These are helpful to all children, but particularly those who may have experienced trauma. Incorporating regular mindfulness practices and emotional check-ins can provide children with tools to start to recognise and manage their feelings.

A case study from my work involved a primary school that implemented a trauma-informed approach. This included regular social and emotional literacy (SEL) activities and teacher training on trauma awareness (in this case, in the Service child context). One of the offshoots of this was that some members of the school community started to deal with emotions from their backgrounds. Far from being a hinderance to strategies for support, colleagues suggested that they felt liberated to work with children with authenticity.

The need to address matters of trauma, grief and loss in primary education is an uncomfortable inevitability. By fostering a supportive and empathetic environment, the school community can enhance the wellbeing and outcomes of all children. The practices discussed, while particularly beneficial for specific groups like Service children, are broadly applicable to all children with a view to creating inclusive and authentic educational spaces. By recognising the diverse experiences of trauma and loss and responding with sensitivity and care, practitioners ensure that the impact of these events are met in a manner that cultivates courage, hope and openness.

The earlier children receive help and support, the less likely that a situation will worsen; recognised agencies, both statutory and non-statutory organisations, can offer help and support to children in these circumstances. It is therefore important that we create safe spaces for children to feel supported and secure; some classroom strategies may include:

- incorporating familiar, safe routines in the classroom so children know what to expect;
- providing visual timetables on the wall or miniature ones on the desk so learners know what is going to happen during the day;
- maintaining clear and consistent routines and expectations, especially when it comes to behaviour management;
- consideration of any sensory elements that may be overstimulating such as very bright lights;
- celebrating daily successes, not just in the academic field but in all areas;
- ensuring children feel proud of their work – perhaps have one wall with 30 clipboards on it, one for each child, and always have a piece of work on display on the child's clipboard; perhaps they can also put work up there when they feel very proud of it;

(Continued)

- giving daily space to reflect on how we are feeling, with the teacher also role modelling talking about a range of feelings;
- considering building journalling or reflective diary writing into part of the school week – if children are not able to write, they could draw or colour in to show how they are feeling;
- ensuring a strong partnership is formed between the parents/carers and the teachers – check in with parents and carers about good things that have happened, not just about incidents or accidents.

LINK TO CLASSROOM PRACTICE: FIVE PEOPLE WHO CAN HELP ME

Give each child either a template of a hand print or ask them to draw around their hand. On each of the five fingers, they can write down someone they can talk to or who can help them if they are upset. Model this by creating your own hand template and share with your class who you talk to if you are upset; this will help normalising that adults also need support and can feel lost or sad.

CHILDREN LOOKED AFTER (CLA), CHILDREN IN CARE (CIC) AND CARE-EXPERIENCED CHILDREN

If a child is taken into the care of their local authority for longer than 24 hours they are known as a *child looked after* (CLA), previously titled *looked after children*; a child stops being 'looked after' once they either return to their caregivers, are adopted, or when they turn 18. The title change came about to show the need for a focus on the child and their best interests at the heart of all decisions that are made. CLAs are also often referred to as *children in care* (CIC), a term which many children and young people prefer (NSPCC, 2024).

Local authorities in all four nations in the UK must offer support for care leavers until they reach 21 years old. Many CIC have experienced abuse, neglect or other forms of trauma. It's important that CIC are provided with the care and support they need to be healthy and safe, to have the same opportunities as their peers and, ultimately, to move successfully into adulthood

(NSPCC, 2024). Each of the countries within the UK has a varying understanding of a CLA, but, generally, a CLA is either living with a foster family, living with friends or a relative through kinship foster care, living in a residential home, or living in a residential setting such as a school, secure unit, or secure living accommodation (ibid.).

REFLECTIVE QUESTION 4.2

Think about something or someone you have lost; what are ways you can help yourself accept and deal with the loss?

How might we support children dealing with loss?

The grief which follows the loss of a parent has long been a subject of interest among prominent researchers, who have been intrigued by the pain and consequences of such losses (Lytje and Dyregrov, 2023). The general failure to consider the perspectives of young children is problematic, as current studies indicate that parental bereavement can increase the likelihood of children experiencing depression and increase the likelihood of engaging in high-risk behaviour. Studies have also suggested that the likelihood of the above consequences occurring may be reduced should children receive sufficient support from others. Nevertheless, to provide support, it is necessary to understand both how young children may express their grief and the forms of support that might benefit them (ibid.). Let us explore the topics of grief and bereavement more in the following section.

It is also important for educators to understand that any children or young people who have been or are CLA, or adopted, are living with loss; loss of their birth family connections and loss of their original start in life. Many children experience loss, but it can look different for all, such as death of a family pet, a friend who moves house, or parents splitting up. Children who are in care or adopted have a lifelong loss to live with, that they may not fully understand at a young age. Even children who are adopted as babies still may have a loss, as after nine months of hearing their birth mother's voice through the walls of the womb, they no longer can.

Primary school teachers are in an ideal situation to support children who may be experiencing loss and grief and to prepare all children for future (eventual) experiences of loss. To best offer support to children experiencing loss and to provide anticipatory education to all children, teachers themselves need to 'be prepared' to face loss and grief. As well as being good listeners and good communicators, teachers need to be able to use the language of loss, grief and death easily and naturally. They need to be aware of grief and bereavement patterns and be able to identify and come to terms with their feelings about their own loss experiences. A particularly helpful resource for primary teachers is Ward and associates' *Good Grief* (1995). Most importantly, teachers need to ensure that they have their own support person with whom they can discuss their feelings and thoughts. Supporting a grieving person can touch teachers in unexpected ways and it is important to be able to talk about this with a friend or colleague and to seek professional help if necessary. Organisations such as CRUSE can also help teachers (Milton, 2004).

GRIEF AND BEREAVEMENT

Bereavement refers to the experience of someone close to us dying and leaving us 'bereaved'. Grief is the journey of emotions that we go through as we process the death and loss of the person from our network. Grief is the way in which we adjust to living with a significant loss – it is the pain of 'letting go' (Milton, 2004). Although the subject of death and bereavement is often a 'taboo' subject, the nature and incidence of bereavement is not an issue that practitioners can shy away from (Porter, 2016).

REFLECTIVE QUESTION 4.3

How were you taught about death growing up, and how big a part does death and grieving play in your life now?

In the UK, approximately one in 29 children have experienced the death of a parent or sibling; clearly teachers and schools are in a key position to support with grief provision and the facilitation of these difficult conversations and sharing of coping strategies (Costelloe et al., 2020). However, not much is known about how schools can help children to cope with death and dying. Duncan (2020) found that three key strategies for supporting a child with bereavement – encouraging children to openly communicate; finding comfort in various ways; and expressing emotion regularly – were the most common approaches. The results indicate that if the correct approaches are taken children can feel supported during a challenging and fearful time in their lives (ibid.).

Interestingly, however, a mixed-methods study conducted in the UK on this topic found that providing emotional support to a bereaved child has a negative impact on the emotional wellbeing of staff; therefore, schools must consider how other professionals and agencies, such as educational psychologists (EPs), may be better prepared to offer bereavement support (Costelloe et al., 2020).

LINK TO CLASSROOM PRACTICE: LETTER TO A LOVED ONE

Talk to your class about how, even when we lose people from our network – when they move away or even through death – we can still remember them and cherish the special memories of times that we spent together with them. Encourage them to write a letter, or perhaps a shorter postcard, to the person (or animal) they have lost. They could use these as possible sentence starters:

- My favourite memory with you is ...
- One thing that reminds me of you is ...
- One thing I would love to say to you is ...

Books can also be a useful way to facilitate conversations around death in a more child-friendly way. As with many big concepts in life, using children's literature can be an accessible way for teachers to discuss how characters feel in the book when they lose things, or when they feel sad. Books can be a good stimulus to encourage children to ask questions and discuss concepts such as death and funerals (Milton, 2004).

To unpick this further, next we share a reflection on supporting children who have been bereaved, with a thoughtful contribution from Emma L. Palastanga.

CONTRIBUTION: CHILDREN AND BEREAVEMENT

BY EMMA L. PALASTANGA – AN INDEPENDENT EDUCATOR AND FORMER OFSTED INSPECTOR AND WHO HAS HELD LEADERSHIP ROLES IN PRIMARY SCHOOLS

It is a sad fact that everyone will experience loss at some point in their life. According to Grief Encounter (www.griefencounter.org.uk) one child in every UK classroom will experience bereavement by the time they reach 16 years old. Grief is the response we have to any type of loss, but bereavement is grief that involves the death of a loved one. It is a worrying fact that in a straw poll I conducted 49 per cent stated that their school does not have a bereavement

(Continued)

policy and 12 per cent were unsure if their school did or did not have a policy in place, begging the question as to whether we are doing the best we can to support bereaved children. In this short piece I shall explore the topic of childhood bereavement and offer suggestions of support.

There are many complexities to bereavement: the child and their wider supportive relationships; the relationship between the child and the loved one who has died; the circumstances surrounding the death – was it after a long illness, a sudden death through natural causes or even suicide? In a nutshell, the grief journey will likely be messy and unpredictable, and every bereavement will be unique to the individuals involved. On the one hand, for many children we often assume this loss is likely to be a pet or a grandparent, an elderly relative who has had a 'good life', perhaps not coming as a huge surprise to the family. On the other hand, though, it may well be a significant loss to the child, depending on the bond between them – especially if they lived in the same home or were even a primary caregiver. I have worked with children in primary school at different ages, some who have lost parents, and a child who lost her ten-year-old sister with complex needs, to COVID.

Supporting a bereaved adult, let alone a child, can be challenging for many because people worry they may say 'the wrong thing' – but saying nothing is far worse. Grief can feel very lonely, confusing and complex, especially to a child. Parminder Sahota, Director of Clinical Services for Grief Encounter, says that 'by listening, validating feelings and being present adults can make an impact on children affected by grief'. It is by showing compassion for emotional expression – whether that is tears, anger or seemingly unrelated behavioural changes – making space for grief alongside daily routines and joyous moments and supporting an age-appropriate understanding of death that we can help bereaved children.

While supporting a bereaved child, communication and working alongside the child's primary caregiver is of utmost importance, expressing any concerns from school to home and home to school or asking the parent and child what the child would find helpful if they are able to articulate it. I appreciate that if requests are made for one-to-one support or home education they may not always be possible, but being able to call home at lunchtime if they are distressed or having a quiet space to gather their thoughts might be a useful starting point. Remember too, that some families will take great comfort in their faith at a time of loss, while others may be humanist, atheist or agnostic, for example; so statements such as 'they are in a better place', therefore, may not always be helpful.

I have written mostly about grief in the early days of bereavement, but the importance of understanding that grief is something we learn to live alongside and build our lives around should not be underestimated; it isn't something which fades over time. Anniversaries of the death, religious festivals such as Eid or Christmas and, of course, birthdays, both of the child and the deceased, can be very painful reminders of the loss. Sometimes just a smell, a song or a memory can trigger emotions; understanding this in long-term grief, as well as normalising it can be a great relief to those struggling with it.

I have also focused on grief in the single bereaved person, but this can affect an entire class as they experience mortality, perhaps for the first time; this can trigger feelings of anxiety about their own loved ones. It could be a death in the school community, which will be a shared grief on a larger scale, but just as upsetting for those involved. In this case, perhaps a shared act of condolence such as a memorial garden, a notable tree or a quiet space for reflection for those who knew the deceased could be considered.

In summary, bereavement will affect approximately one in 29 children before they are 16; each person's loss will be felt differently depending on a number of factors, but the compassion and empathy shown by others, both adults and classmates, will help children in this vulnerable state to navigate one of life's most complex experiences.

LINK TO CLASSROOM PRACTICE: FEELINGS FIRST AID BOX

Talk to the class about how, when we are physically hurt, we can use the items in a first aid box to help make us better, such as antiseptic wipes and plasters. Now think about when we feel sad, or lost, or are grieving. What could we put in a feelings first aid box to make us feel better? You may wish to make physical boxes – for example, children could bring in a shoe box and fill it with items that bring joy – or they could do this abstractly using a template of a box and drawing or listing things in it that cheer them up, such as a favourite drink, snack, snuggly blanket, or teddy.

UNDERSTANDING TRAUMA

Clearly, whether we're supporting children who have suffered loss, bereavement, abuse or other ACEs, there is a need for teachers and schools to understand trauma. If a school or setting has a trauma-informed approach, the institution realises the widespread impact of trauma and understands potential paths for recovery. Trauma-informed care (TIC) and trauma-informed practice (TIP) are approaches to caring for children and young people who have experienced ACEs and traumatic events during their lives. This chapter concludes with a thoughtful reflection from Louise Lawton and Rebecca Tarplett on the need for educators to have a better understanding of trauma and the impact of trauma on children's lives, and how TIP should be utilised in all schools and settings.

CONTRIBUTION: TRAUMA, CHILDHOOD AND THE LASTING LEGACY FOR ADULTHOOD

BY LOUISE LAWTON AND REBECCA TARPLETT (TICK HUB) – TRAINED TRAUMA-INFORMED PRACTITIONERS WHO HAVE WORKED IN SCHOOLS FOR NEARLY 20 YEARS

'Trauma' is a term we have become more familiar with in schools – certainly in the last few years. With a growing body of research and knowledge about trauma, terms such as 'trauma-informed practice' are becoming more common. Educators know that the effects of trauma can be evident in children and can certainly be seen in the classroom. We also know that trauma goes on to affect the adult years, if left untreated. But what is trauma? Do we, as teachers, have enough knowledge about it?

Trauma is different in every case. It is, essentially, the body's response to a perceived threat to survival or emotional wellbeing of an individual and it can be broken down into two elements that need to be present for trauma to occur. These are:

- an external event, incident or threat to a person;
- an internal response to that threat, which will vary depending on many factors.

When trauma occurs this leads to adverse brain, bodily and/or psychological changes that can damage oneself, including the person's ability to develop relationships, which, in turn, can lead to an impact on and impairment of their ability to live fully, learn and work.

Crucially, we know that children are more vulnerable to trauma than adults; this is because they are more likely to absorb experiences at a younger age.

The same sponge-like properties that enable our brain to absorb experiences such as language in the first three years of our life also absorb:

- chaos
- threat
- fear

with the same facility as absorbing language.

(Perry, 2019)

When children experience trauma there can be a range of barriers from these unresolved experiences. These can include, but are not limited to, the effects that trauma has on their ability to make relationships, to explore the world around them, their emotional health and wellbeing. It can also impact on their sleeping patterns and eating habits – all of which then have lasting impacts on their development. We must not forget the physical effects of trauma. Trauma can put a child (or adult) into a fight, flight or freeze scenario – these physical effects can lead to things like children having a higher resting pulse and higher cortisol levels – which can lead to them normalising trauma responses to abnormal situations.

Geddes (2022) explored the brain's development and talked about typical brain organisation – where the logical brain is in the majority at the top of the upside-down pyramid; emotional and relational brain in the middle section, and the survival brain is in the minority at the bottom third of the upside-down pyramid – allowing children to make sensible decisions. When trauma occurs, the impacts are long lasting – not only affecting a person's mental health, but also creating long-lasting barriers to learning and education. Children who experience trauma are more likely to have slower growth, both physically and intellectually; they are more likely to avoid taking managed learning risks because

(Continued)

they are hyper vigilant; they often have lower self-esteem than their emotionally secure peers; and have less control of their impulses.

So, as teachers, we have a role to play. TIP means that we recognise how traumatic experiences impact lives and seek to understand how this has an impact on learning and behaviour. We proactively create safe and caring learning environments; more widely, it involves strategic planning, staff training, refreshing policies to reflect this practice and direct intervention to support young people's wellbeing and happiness while at school. After all, a happy child will be ready to learn. We need to give our young people the best possible opportunities to thrive and not just survive.

SUMMARY

- Classrooms must be safe, inclusive spaces where children and young people feel comfortable and supported to talk about their feelings.
- ACEs can cause toxic stress, impacting the brain and affecting how the body responds to stress; however, preventing early trauma can improve adult mental health. ACEs can negatively affect holistic development; individuals with ACEs are more prone to developing mental and physical health problems later in life.
- Those working with children must receive regular training in safeguarding to remain updated with workplace safeguarding and protection policies, as well as safeguarding officers' names and telephone numbers. Most importantly, teachers need to ensure that they have their own support person with whom they can discuss their feelings and thoughts. Supporting a grieving person can touch teachers in unexpected ways and it is important to be able to talk about this with a friend or colleague and to seek professional help if necessary.

5

DEPRESSION AND ANXIETY

INTRODUCTION

We are seeing higher levels of depression, anxiety and self-harm in children than ever before. How can we support children who may need nurturing with their mental health and wellbeing in the classroom? This chapter explores some of the literature and research around young people's mental health, with a focus on supporting children with depression and anxiety, sharing four thoughtful contributions from experienced professionals.

CHILDREN'S EMOTIONS

Before looking more closely at symptoms and support of depression and anxiety in children, let us consider children's emotions with this thoughtful introduction from Nimrita Bahia, Course Director, Lecturer and Deputy Designated Safeguarding Lead, at Coventry University.

> Emotions are like animals:
>
> No two are quite the same.
>
> Some are gentle; others, fierce;
>
> And some are hard to tame.
>
> (De Botton, 2023)

Children's experiences of emotions are not only vast; they can also vary in intensity and in how often they surface. Children as young as two years can distinguish an emotion (Dunn et al., 1987); they acquire an understanding of emotions, even if only at a basic level, through their acts of pretend play and responses observed to emotional cues in others (Widen and Russell, 2008). There is a thriving body of children's literature which encourages harnessing emotional literacy, self-regulation and management of emotions through creative, illustrative endeavours to support parents, carers and educators. Although there is a move towards becoming more open and endorsing of 'talking about feelings', a cautious attitude continues to pervade in accepting that children can and do experience significant presentations of anxiety, which may be identified as dispositions. For example, 8–11 per cent of children as young as five to six years experience anxiety (Mental Health Foundation, 2023).

Emotions comprising fear, worry, or upset can follow in presenting as behaviours to include irritability, clinginess and/or distress, suggestive of both a child's inability to regulate a feeling and also their need for comfort and support in managing the emotion. While these can be prompted by a single experience, for some children these can be repeated and thus observed as a pattern – likely reactions triggered by their lived experiences of family and school life. Typically, a child's reaction of anxiety or sustained anxiety (anxious disposition), can be pre-empted by parental marital conflict, parental ill health within the family home, bullying, peer/friendship conflict, worry of exams/tests or academic performance in school. However, practices of adult others – including parents, carers and educators – to exhibit excessive control, or dramatic reactions in an attempt to discipline the child can further intensify a child's fear and worry and thus exacerbate anxiety.

A child's default means of processing a situation which pre-empts anxiety is likely to be *internal* – for example, this is my fault; they are likely unable to compartmentalise, as adults might, to manage responsibility for experiences. This can have far-reaching impacts on a child's feeling of wellbeing (Weis et al., 2016; Leerkes and Augustine, 2019) and also on their socio-emotional development, which in turn fosters school readiness (Harrington et al, 2020). It is thus critical, as educators, to appreciate that children are intrinsically sensitive to both their surroundings (that is, what is happening around them in a given space) and observed emotions – and thus transactions – between them and others (such as what others say in response to them, how often and in response to which questions, comments); it is in this way that they learn to navigate the world. Our endeavours to understand their anxiety must begin with fostering values which enable them to feel *safe*, *comforted* and *permitted* to be their authentic self.

HOW DO WE DEFINE ANXIETY AND DEPRESSION?

Let's take a closer look at what we mean by the terms 'depression' and 'anxiety'.

DEPRESSION

Depression can turn into a long-term problem as it involves very low mood that results in loss of interest or pleasure in daily life.

REFLECTIVE QUESTION 5.1

How would you define depression?

When do you think low mood becomes depression, and how can we ascertain when the low mood is becoming an issue?

Some possible signs of depression in children may include:

- sadness, or a low mood that does not go away
- being irritable or grumpy all the time
- not being interested in things they used to enjoy
- feeling tired and exhausted a lot of the time (NHS, 2023b).

These feelings can translate into problems such as trouble sleeping, lack or inability to concentrate, reduced socialisation and indecisiveness. Children with depression may also have issues with food, either overeating or undereating, and thus have changes in weight. A young person with depression may also have thoughts about suicide, or self-harming, or actually self-harm, such as cutting their skin or taking an overdose (ibid.). Young people who are depressed may misuse drugs or alcohol.

So, why do children become depressed? Things that increase the risk of depression in children include:

- family difficulties, such as parental divorce
- bullying at school
- physical, emotional or sexual abuse
- a family history of depression or other mental health problems (ibid.).

Depression may be triggered by an event such as death of a family member, or some children may be more disposed to depression through genetics for example.

SEASONAL AFFECTIVE DISORDER (SAD)

There is another type of depression you may be familiar with – or perhaps consider you suffer with yourself: seasonal affective disorder (SAD). SAD is a type of depression that comes at certain times of the year, often experienced in winter when days are shorter and darker; interestingly, hotter temperatures and summer can lead to SAD also. Many people have favourite and least favourite seasons; however, SAD may be to blame if a person is feeling low for a significant period of time (Young Minds, 2024).

ANXIETY

Although it is normal to feel anxious or worried at times, anxiety can become a problem when it begins to interfere with daily actions.

REFLECTIVE QUESTION 5.2

Have you experienced anxiety and, if so, what helped you to regain control in that moment? What situations at school do you think may make children feel more anxious?

Generalised anxiety disorder (GAD) refers to when an individual experiences excessive anxiety and worry (apprehensive expectation), occurring more days than not for at least six months, about a number of events or activities (such as work or school performance). People with anxiety find it difficult, or impossible, to control their feelings of worry and this may present through the following possible symptoms:

- feeling restless
- being easily fatigued
- difficulty concentrating or mind going blank
- irritability
- muscle tension
- sleep disturbance (difficulty falling or staying asleep, or restless unsatisfying sleep) (Substance Abuse and Mental Health Services Administration, 2016).

One way that is shown to help regain control when feeling very anxious is through breathing; focusing on our breathing brings our attention fully into the present and helps us take back control of our body, restoring balance.

LINK TO CLASSROOM PRACTICE: BOX BREATHING

This is a great exercise to use with your class to offer space for a mindful moment throughout the busy school day, and also to do with a child if they need coregulation at a time of stress or upset.

This exercise is called the *box breath* because you can imagine drawing a square as you breathe in, hold, breathe out, and hold:

- *side 1 of the square*: breathe in and count up to four slowly;
- *side 2 of the square*: hold your inheld breath for four seconds;
- *side 3 of the square*: slowly exhale through your mouth for four seconds;
- *side 4 of the square*: hold your empty lungs for four seconds;
- *repeat* the above steps until you feel recentred.

This will help you slow down your breathing. It works by distracting your mind and calming the nervous system.

In the following contribution from Charlotte Costello, we consider how we can support children with daily anxiety, and the importance of creating manageable plans.

CONTRIBUTION: ANXIETY IN CHILDREN

BY CHARLOTTE COSTELLO – SENIOR SEN TEACHING ASSISTANT

Anxiety in children presents itself in many different forms and is more noticeable in some children than it is in others. There is no specific age at which anxiety disorders 'peak' in terms of severity. Being able to spot the signs of anxiety in a child and creating solutions can make a child's experience in education much more positive and less daunting.

As a senior SEN teaching assistant, anxiety in children is something that I come across every day; spotting the signs is the first step to creating a manageable plan for the child, a plan that the child and parents/carers are a part of creating. Some children have an anxiety that is triggered by the school setting; others have anxiety that happens outside school, but they do not yet know the triggers.

Some of the obvious signs that a child has anxiety can be:

- eating less or more than usual;
- getting bad stomach aches and feeling sick on a regular basis;
- constant refusal to do a task and walking away (sometimes refusing to sit in a classroom or in a certain area of the class);
- picking at skin or clothing;
- struggling to catch their breath when very overwhelmed.

(Continued)

These are just a few signs that you may spot in a child that has anxiety – some may be harder to spot as the child may mask the signs. If you know a child well these signs will be easier to recognise.

Creating a manageable plan is a key part in being able to support the child. Building a trusting relationship with the child will make a huge impact because you need to create that *go-to* person who they feel is their safe space and trusted person.

Sometimes it is very hard for the young person to understand their triggers and what makes them feel anxious; understanding your emotions as a young person and sometimes as an adult can be difficult and overwhelming. We need to remind them that this is OK; it is OK to feel different emotions and that it is how we respond to these emotions that is important.

If the triggers are not known, create a coping mechanism for when they are feeling anxious.

If the child recognises the triggers that cause their anxiety a plan can be put into place to help them deal with the cause of the anxiety and understand how they feel when they have these triggers and what strategies help them best.

LINK TO CLASSROOM PRACTICE: THREE THINGS

To reflect on this contribution, Charlotte offers another classroom exercise to try: the 3–3–3 rule.

- Ask your child to name three things that they can see
- Then three sounds they can hear
- Then move three different parts of their body.

This mindfulness strategy will help a child engage their senses and focus on the reality rather than concentrate on what may happen. Strategies like this can help when supporting a child with anxiety; these practices are best for the trusted adult to do alongside the child as they will be able to mirror what you are doing.

COMORBIDITY OF ANXIETY AND DEPRESSION

Often, people with anxiety may also have depression; we call this being *comorbid*. Experiencing both anxiety and depression contributes to worse psychosocial function and quality of life (Hopwood, 2023). The 5th edition of the *Diagnostic and Statistical Manual of Mental Disorders* (DSM-5; APA, 2013) introduced the *anxious distress* specifier to identify patients with major depressive disorder (MDD) and comorbid anxiety. It can sometimes be difficult to discern whether anxiety triggers depression or depression triggers anxiety (Hopwood, 2023).

STRATEGIES TO SUPPORT ANXIETY AND DEPRESSION

Young Minds (2024) recommend four ways to help one feel better:

- talk to someone you trust;
- get creative;
- stay active;
- try mindfulness or meditation.

Look at your school weekly timetable; are there spaces and times throughout the week where children could action all four of these strategies? Some simple ideas for each of these four ways are suggested below.

Talk to someone you trust

Could children have a peer or buddy in a different class or older year group as someone to talk to? Could there be a *talking box* on your desk where children could insert a note with their name on if they wanted to have a chat with you?

Get creative

Expressing ourselves through arts, music, dance or movement can help us process feelings, so consider where there are opportunities in the day such as yoga, singing or art and clay activities for 'golden time' opportunities or free choice?

Stay active

Are there any opportunities for brain breaks in the day, a chance for a mental reset as you get the class to stand up and play 'Simon says' between lessons?

Being outdoors can have great benefits on our mental health; can you move any activities out into the playground to add further activity?

Try mindfulness or meditation

Factor in five minutes at the start or end of the day to enjoy listening to a short meditation video online with the lights off, or play a piece of calming music when children are packing their bags, or set out mindful colouring for playtimes (see further mindfulness ideas in Chapter 13).

In the following contribution, Simon Turnnidge offers an overview of seven strategies that can be used to support children and young people with depression or/and anxiety.

CONTRIBUTION: APPROACHES TO MANAGING ANXIETY AND DEPRESSION IN CHILDREN

BY SIMON TURNNIDGE – EXECUTIVE HEADTEACHER OF ST AUBYN AND POPLAR ADOLESCENT UNIT, THERAPEUTIC EDUCATION DEPARTMENTS

Effectively managing anxiety and depression in children requires a multifaceted approach that addresses the child's emotional, social and cognitive needs. Here are some key strategies.

Early identification and intervention: early recognition of symptoms is crucial for effective management. The NHS and Public Health England (PHE) emphasise the importance of regular mental health check-ups and open communication with children. Being attentive to changes in behaviour or mood can help identify issues early.

Psychotherapy: Cognitive behavioural therapy (CBT) is a highly effective form of therapy for children with anxiety and depression. The UK's National Institute for Health and Care Excellence (NICE) recommends CBT as the first-line treatment for mild to moderate cases of anxiety and depression in children. It helps children recognise negative thought patterns, develop coping strategies and build resilience. Other therapeutic approaches, such as play therapy, art therapy and family therapy, can also be beneficial.

Dialectical behaviour therapy (DBT) skills: originally developed for adults, this has been adapted for children and adolescents to help manage intense emotions and improve coping skills. DBT focuses on four main skill sets:

- *mindfulness*: teaching children to be present and aware of their emotions without judgement. Mindfulness exercises can help children focus on the here and now, reducing anxiety about past or future events;

- *distress tolerance*: helping children develop skills to tolerate and cope with distressing situations without resorting to harmful behaviours. Techniques such as TIPP (temperature; intense exercise; paced breathing; progressive relaxation) can be useful in managing immediate anxiety or stress;
- *emotion regulation*: assisting children in understanding and managing their emotions effectively, including identifying emotions, reducing vulnerability to negative emotions and increasing positive emotional experiences;
- *interpersonal effectiveness*: building skills to communicate effectively, maintain relationships and set healthy boundaries. This is particularly important for children with social anxiety or those struggling with peer relationships.

Parental support and education: educating parents and carers about anxiety and depression is essential for creating a supportive home environment. Charities like Young Minds and Place2Be offer resources and training for parents to help them support their child's mental health. Parents should be encouraged to listen actively, validate their child's feelings and model healthy coping strategies. Establishing routines, ensuring a balanced diet and promoting regular physical activity can also help.

Medication: in some cases, medication may be necessary, particularly for moderate to severe anxiety and depression. Antidepressants, such as selective serotonin reuptake inhibitors (SSRIs), can be prescribed under the guidance of a child psychiatrist. However, NICE guidelines suggest that medication is typically considered after other interventions have been explored.

School support: schools play a vital role in supporting children's mental health. According to the DfE in the UK, teachers and school counsellors should be aware of the signs of anxiety and depression and create an inclusive and supportive environment. Providing accommodations, such as modified assignments or additional time for tests, can help alleviate academic pressure. The UK government's Green Paper on *Transforming Children and Young People's Mental Health Provision* (DfE, 2017) highlights the importance of having a designated mental health lead in every school.

Mindfulness and relaxation techniques: encouraging children to practise mindfulness, deep breathing exercises, and relaxation techniques can help them manage stress and anxiety. The Mindfulness in Schools Project in the UK has shown positive results in improving emotional regulation and reducing anxiety in children through mindfulness-based programmes (DfE, 2017).

In this next chapter contribution, Rose Carter offers a tutor's perspective on supporting children with anxiety and highlights the importance of a possible relationship between adult and child.

CONTRIBUTION: CHILDREN AND ANXIETY – A TUTOR'S PERSPECTIVE

BY ROSE CARTER, BSC PGCE (QTS) – FOUNDER, CE, AND PROFESSIONAL TUTOR AT INSPIRES TUITION

The majority of children and young people that are referred either by parents or schools have some level of anxiety and trauma. This is often in combination with another diagnosis such as ASD/ADHD. The approach used is trauma-informed and child-led. This ensures that the child is not overwhelmed. When children are referred, they are at the bottom of Maslow's hierarchy of needs, looking for safety; this lack of connection and self-esteem exacerbates their anxiety and means that it is difficult for them to grow.

It is our job, as educators, to work with children to help them feel secure and gain self-esteem; to help them be the best they can be – socially, emotionally and academically. This means that before meeting the young person for the first time it is important to gather all information – for example, EHCP, prior teacher reports, education psychologist reports and, most importantly, to speak to parents/carers. From this you can then work out the approach for the first meeting.

The approach I use can vary – sometimes it is very gentle, quiet and calm, at other times it is loud and blunt. Humour is very important in tuition sessions; we laugh a lot! I let my personality shine through as it's really important for the child to see you as a person (they also call me by my first name, not surname).

During the first session (usually playing a game of Uno™) we discuss what the child is good at and not so good at. We do not do anything academic unless the child initiates it. The most important part of a first meeting is understanding that it is the beginning of building a relationship and assessing how the child learns. This includes listening very closely to their wants and needs and working out a curriculum with them helps to take ownership of their learning, therefore reducing anxiety.

With regard to behaviour, it is important to be assertive but not authoritarian and to set boundaries but not be too rigid. As you get to know the child it will be easier to spot the triggers and work with them to understand and manage their own behavioural choices. Sleep and food have a big part to play in mood. If a child comes to school tired and hungry, they are less likely to want to engage. I always ask at the beginning of a session how they've slept. I always carry snacks! This also shows care. Many of the children and young people who are referred to me by schools are on free school meals, therefore food (or lack of) is an important part of their day.

As the relationship with the young person grows and they begin to trust you their anxiety reduces and their sense of self-worth increases. This means that they start exploring new ideas and are much more open to finding different methods of learning. This then improves their mood and their anxiety reduces further; they then understand the purpose of what they're doing and why they're doing it.

As a final thought, we need to bear in mind that if we don't pay attention to helping children feel safe and connected to the people around them, they will not flourish – in fact they may sink. That is why building a relationship, showing care and encouraging trust are so essential.

LINK TO CLASSROOM PRACTICE: HOW TO JOURNAL

Some children may find journalling useful as a way to write down feelings and ideas that they are not ready to share out loud. It could be a good idea to raid the school stationery cupboard at the end of term and find any of the odd exercise books no one needed or the old design exercise books that had lines that were too small, etc.! Give each child one of these empty books and encourage them to decorate the book. Role model that journalling may involve writing down feelings and events like a diary, or can simply be a space to draw, doodle, or note down important things from the day. Many adults find that journalling helps them to feel less stressed as they reflect on their feelings, so helping them develop a skill like keeping a journal may be something they take forward for life.

MENTAL HEALTH BEFORE AND DURING COVID

One question we are still trying to answer is to what extent the COVID lockdowns of 2020 have affected the children and young people who experienced them.

REFLECTIVE QUESTION 5.3

Do you think there are still repercussions of the COVID lockdowns on children and young people's mental health?

How may these lockdowns have affected levels of depression and anxiety?

The follow-up of England's Mental Health of Children and Young People (MHCYP) survey provides a rare resource on what the pandemic has meant for children (Newlove-Delgado et al., 2021). This study showed that the rising level of issues with mental health that was reported in adults was also represented in children and young people aged five to 16 years old in England, with the incidence rising from 10·8 per cent in 2017 to 16·0 per cent in July 2020 across age, gender, and ethnic groups (ibid.) Some other key findings were:

- during the pandemic, young women had the highest prevalence of probable mental health problems (27·2 per cent);
- more than a quarter of children (aged five to 16 years) and young people (aged 17–22) reported disrupted sleep and one in ten (5·4 per cent of children and 13·8 per cent of young people) often or always felt lonely;
- both problems were more common in those with probable mental health problems, of whom 18·0 per cent felt fearful of leaving the house because of COVID-19;
- children with a parent in psychological distress were more likely to have a probable mental health problem (ibid.).

These findings remind us of the importance of support for parents and carers so that they can in turn support their children; we need to foster positive home–school partnerships to help children to thrive. In this final contribution of the chapter, Erin Skelton reminds us of the importance of connections and communication.

CONTRIBUTION: THE ROOT OF ANXIETY

BY ERIN SKELTON – CHIEF STRATEGY OFFICER AT BRIGHT FIELD CONSULTING AND A TEACHER OF PSYCHOLOGY, CRIMINOLOGY AND RELIGIOUS STUDIES AT WORKSOP COLLEGE

Anxiety in school-aged children is a complex issue and one that teachers, CAMHS professionals, parents and schools struggle to find a solution to. This issue is compounded by an often-contradictory body of advice, mental health services bowing under the weight of current need and government benchmarks that focus school targets on attendance and performance. Although this paints a damning picture of how we approach anxiety in our students, it also must be said that as a society we better understand the correlating factors that make children and teenagers more vulnerable to anxiety and depression than ever before. In my experience as a designated safeguarding lead (DSL), Head of KS4 and Head of Sixth Form over the years, I have observed patterns to the anxiety in my pupils.

Attachment style is an influencing factor in student anxiety. Students who have avoidant, and in some cases ambivalent, attachment styles are often task-focused and performance-driven. They often believe that love is transactional and validation is external. Many anxious students with avoidant attachment styles live in households where parents are emotionally unavailable or emotionally abusive. Similarly, students with ambivalent attachment styles often come from households where parenting lacks clear boundaries, is inconsistent or unreliable. My experience is that many of these parents often display signs of their own ACEs, but have struggled to break that cycle in their own parenting; love becomes an external validation of academic or extra-curricular performance. In selective independent schools, this situation is often intensified by two additional factors. Firstly, many parents of children with avoidant attachment styles are themselves high-performing perfectionists. This often drives anxiety in their children in their attempts to academically perform as well as their parents in, arguably, a far more challenging educational landscape than that of their

(Continued)

parents. Secondly, many parents of children with avoidant attachment styles in selective independent schools are highly directive with GCSE and A level choices as well as university course and provider, ultimately giving the student little choice in what they study – the narrative being that the parent is paying for secondary education and university.

Family anxiety and parenting style has an impact on school-aged children. A recent study by Professor Eley at the Institute of Psychiatry, Psychology and Neuroscience at King's College London found that, despite genetic influences on anxiety, living in an anxious environment is more likely to cause anxiety in young people (Eley, 2015). Furthermore, a 2021 study found that students who live in households where their mother has depression are more likely to also suffer from depression, whereas in households where their father has depression, this is more likely to affect school performance (Brophy et al., 2021). There have also been recent studies which indicate a possible link between parenting styles and the presence of self-injuring behaviours in young people (Burešová et al., 2015).

Gen A are hyperconnected and hyperaware of the world around them. They access and consume information across a vast range of platforms and mediums. They are constantly challenged to understand what might be disinformation or misinformation and there is little regard for their emotional readiness in what they can freely access. In their lifetime, they have experienced a global pandemic, invasions, arguably the greatest calls for equity and equality in the last century, divisive political ideology and a growing acknowledgement of the climate crisis. Their current future is one where there is little certainty. In this landscape, it is natural that our students have increased levels of anxiety and it's our obligation as teachers, parents and policy makers to educate, advocate and make significant change that will directly affect their futures.

Anxiety is not gender specific, but society demonstrates gender biases in how it views and approaches anxiety in boys. Boys still tend to be labelled as underperforming, having poor behaviour or anger management issues when in reality they are highly anxious. They are also less likely to disclose issues around their emotional wellbeing or mental health in environments where they are exposed to toxic masculinity, making getting the right support for our boys a challenge.

Generational and cultural stigma has a significant impact on student anxiety. Many of my students over the years have struggled with the complexity of family beliefs and expectations and their emerging self. Gender, sexual orientation, neurodiversity, mental health and aspirations for the future are just a few of the issues that many students feel they cannot discuss at home for fear of stigma, withdrawal of love or in extreme cases being cut off. This often drives anxiety and issues around conformity and authenticity. This is compounded in sixth form by the complexities of financing a degree or housing. It can also lead to a suppression of need, a miscommunication and a lack of support or diagnosis.

My advice on how to best support our anxious children in our classrooms and schools is that teachers and pastoral staff need to work as a part of a home–school–student triad as advocates for our students, supporting them in mediating when it is needed and ensuring that parents have the support to ensure that home and school are harmonious places which best support the individual student.

The most successful school settings I have worked in to support students with anxiety start at the root cause, offering parental education on a range of relevant topics, having outstanding PSHE, safeguarding and emotional wellbeing provision, a strong student mentoring programme and an excellent pastoral team that knows how to competently navigate external support for the students when this is needed. If money can be found, then it should be spent on student coaching and counselling provision which also runs family sessions to ensure that the students can start to build a toolkit to support their emotional wellbeing as they move through school and beyond.

SUMMARY

- Anxiety and depression can manifest in physical symptoms, such as headaches and stomach aches.
- Problems at school and problem behaviour can be a sign of depression in children and young people.
- Often, people with anxiety may also have depression, we call this being comorbid.
- One way that is shown to help regain control when feeling very anxious is through breathing; focusing on our breathing brings our attention fully into the present and helps us take back control of our body, restoring balance.
- Understanding anxiety and depression in children is vital for promoting their mental health and wellbeing.

6

CHILDREN AND NEURODIVERGENCE

INTRODUCTION

This chapter defines 'neurodivergence' and 'neurodiversity' and discusses how there is a wide range of neurodivergent (ND) conditions, many of which may be comorbid in a learner which can make educational support and inclusivity sometimes feel more challenging. We focus in greater detail on autism and attention deficit hyperactivity disorder (ADHD) as two of the more commonly diagnosed ND conditions, discussing how best to support these forms of neurodiversity in the classroom.

WHAT IS NEURODIVERSITY?

I'm sure that you have heard the term 'neurodiversity' before, but what does it really mean? Perhaps you have been diagnosed as ND yourself or consider that you may be ND, but haven't yet been assessed. It is likely that you may know people in your network who are ND.

REFLECTIVE QUESTION 6.1

What does neurodiversity mean to you?

Which conditions do you feel come under this term?

Neurodivergence isn't a mental health condition or disability – it's a cognitive difference; therefore neurodiversity is just another form of human diversity, referring to our acceptance that each of us has a brain that works in a different way to each other.

Celebrating neurodiversity is about fostering a society of inclusion and support to ensure that those people that are ND are not excluded or judged for conditions that are out of their control. While the concept of neurodiversity seems a rather recent one, for decades we have seen the request for disability advocates to reframe disability as *difference*, not as a deficit (Mullins, 2024), and in this way we should understand that having a ND condition is just a difference in the working of the brain and the resulting thinking and behaviours.

WHAT DOES IT MEAN TO BE NEUROTYPICAL OR NEURODIVERGENT?

The term 'neurodivergent' (ND) is given to someone whose neural pathways work in a different way to someone classed as 'neurotypical' (NT), an abbreviation of 'neurologically typical'. We see the majority of people in society as being neurotypical, meaning they have 'typical' neurological development and performance; those whose brains 'diverge' from the typical functioning are therefore ND, functioning in a different way.

Because neurodiversity is not a medical diagnosis, there is not one definitive list of conditions under this umbrella term – however, the following would likely be included: autism, ADHD, learning disabilities such as dyslexia, dyscalculia, dysgraphia and dyspraxia, developmental language disorder, fragile x syndrome and Tourette syndrome (Cook, 2024).

People who have certain mental health conditions, such as bipolar disorder, obsessive-compulsive disorder (OCD) and anxiety disorders, or intellectual disability such as Down syndrome might also identify as neurodiverse (Children's Hospital Colorado, 2024).

REFLECTIVE QUESTION 6.2

What do you feel are some of the difficulties and challenges in diagnosing neurodivergence in children?

In terms of children, current statistics suggest approximately one in seven children in the UK are ND (Kent Community Health NHS Foundation Trust, 2024), approximately 15 per cent; however, there are complexities when it comes to diagnosis as some of the behavioural traits associated with particular ND conditions can also simply be behaviours exhibited due to age and maturation in NT children. For example, many young children seem to have lots of energy and find it hard to focus, which are also signs of ADHD (ibid.), hence why many practitioners will not diagnose ADHD until at least six years of age.

Additionally, there are many different ND conditions and it is important to note that many of these are comorbid with each other. This can make diagnosis and treatment even more complex, especially in children where their self-reports and assessments may be challenging due to difficulties in communication and understanding. It is for this reason that we as teachers and teacher educators must ensure we are as informed as possible when it comes to recognising, understanding and supporting those children who are ND.

REFLECTIVE QUESTION 6.3

Have you ever hidden or 'masked' who you are in a certain situation?

What do you think masking might look like for ND children who are trying to act like their peers, and what might the ripple effects of masking be on their behaviour and identity?

A familiar term in ND literature is that of 'masking', also known as 'camouflaging', where children try to mimic other people's behaviours and quell their natural instincts in order to 'fit in' to their classroom or social setting. Often, once the child returns home they can remove the behaviour 'mask', which may lead to eruptions of anger or poor behaviour as they cope with the exhaustion from having to contain their behaviours all day. As a result, we can see that children with a ND condition may be more likely to experience anxiety and stress (Kent Community Health NHS Foundation Trust, 2024). Waiting lists for diagnosis may be long, and parents and carers should be encouraged to speak to their school's special educational needs and disabilities coordinator (SENDCo). Many ND young people may have endured negative experiences in childhood; different sensory and cognitive profiles can contribute to vulnerability to these negative experiences and trauma responses (Quinton et al., 2024).

BEING NEURODIVERSITY AFFIRMING

The European Union Council recommended that schools deliver inclusive education, convey common values and promote active citizenship while transmitting a sense of belonging and responding to the diverse needs of learners (European Council, 2018). A common misunderstanding is that neurodiversity is a synonym for special educational needs and disabilities (SEND), but confusing the two leads to misconceptions around the potential of students who are ND (Cook, 2024).

In contrast to this, Grant (2023) talks about the term 'neurodiversity affirming': a 'belief and commitment' in our approach to respecting each individual and not trying to shape them to conform to fit into our education system or societal constructs. But is this really such an easy task? While we understand that neurodiversity is a natural form of human diversity, sometimes we may argue as educators that the curriculums (and hidden curriculums!) in schools push for rigid conformity in the name of standardised assessment on local, national and global levels, and accountability to global league tables such as the Programme for International Student Assessment (PISA). PISA is a worldwide study by the Organisation for Economic Co-operation and Development (OECD) that compares countries globally in terms of outcomes.

Educators are caught between a rock and a hard place when it comes to balancing inclusive education and creative pedagogies with these external assessment pressures and regulatory frameworks (Cook, 2024). What we need to do is strip back teaching to being about the learners and promoting inclusion for all; we can only include all when we really get to know who our students are.

LINK TO CLASSROOM PRACTICE: MANUAL OF ME

This activity is a great way to get to know your class and what they think about themselves. Encourage each member of the class to create a 'manual' all about themselves. There are templates you can find online, or you could create your own, or just give the learners free rein of their design by giving them blank paper to create their manual. Role model through showing a manual you have made about yourself, including possible ideas such as your hobbies, interests, strengths and ways you learn best.

In the first of two contributions in this chapter, David Mather offers a reflection on how to foster this inclusive and affirming environment for ND learners.

CONTRIBUTION: EMBRACING NEURODIVERSITY IN THE PRIMARY EDUCATION CONTEXT

BY DAVID MATHER – SENIOR LECTURER IN EDUCATIONAL LEADERSHIP AND MANAGEMENT, UNIVERSITY OF PORTSMOUTH

Acknowledging and embracing neurodiversity is a matter of championing the perspectives and qualities that children with and without that label bring to the classroom. This involves a conscious shift from viewing neurodivergence as *otherness* to celebrating it as part of diversity and inclusion. My personal journey as a parent to two ND children, including one with an autism diagnosis and an education, health and care (EHC) plan, has highlighted the importance of this cultural (and emotional) shift.

Language, representation and visibility play important roles in developing an inclusive school culture. As a parent advocating for my sons, I have seen first hand how the words we use and the examples we set influence the holistic understanding of neurodiversity. Creating an inclusive school culture requires a whole-school approach, involving parents, carers, teachers, support staff and governors in the school's mission, vision and values. This collaboration and the resulting plan to embed adaptive practices as a norm at every level of the school community can contribute to a culture of care and compassion. This contrasts with a culture of 'tolerance' – something that acknowledges the existence of the ND child but does little else.

To create an environment that truly includes neurodiverse children, practical strategies can be implemented. From my experiences, inclusive practices such as visual day-plans, sensory-enabled classrooms and linear instruction (verbal and written) can be effective. In addition, creating quiet spaces for *any* child who may feel overwhelmed by sensory input can help children and those responsible for nurturing them learn the cues as to when overload occurs (with a view to exploring strategies to address this). School leaders are always central to implementing policy as they have the strategic and operational oversight that turns policy into practice. A planned set of tasks and activities should be visible to all concerned when addressing matters of inclusivity. Furthermore, children to whom these tasks and activities might apply should be collaborators in their formation, thus cultivating authentic leadership practices throughout the school community.

One case study from my experience involves a primary school that implemented a whole-school approach to embracing neurodiversity. This involved training sessions that were co-created by school leaders, neurotypical and ND children and a parent-governor. Delivered over a series of weeks, the sessions addressed school culture and ethos regarding neurodiversity in the first instance; syndicates of teachers and support colleagues devised and shared the approaches to neuro-inclusivity that they wished to try. The notion of 'trying' approaches helped to cultivate curiosity and 'the courage to ask questions' – a mantra that I have since held onto and now incorporate into training sessions that I deliver in relation to equality, diversity and inclusion.

In conclusion, embracing neurodiversity in the primary school community has transformative potential. By valuing all forms of neurodiversity and fostering an inclusive culture, schools can enhance the wellbeing and outcomes of children and adults alike.

LINK TO CLASSROOM PRACTICE: VISUAL TIMETABLES

Many classrooms have timetables displayed on the wall. If you're a teacher or teaching assistant, consider if you have a timetable up in your classroom. What does it look like? Is it words or pictures? How accessible is it? Could some children benefit from having personal versions of the timetable on their desk so they can clearly see what is coming up throughout the day, perhaps ticking the subjects and activities off as they complete them?

COMMON BEHAVIOURS IN CHILDREN WITH ND CONDITIONS

Let us zoom in on two ND conditions, ASD and ADHD. It often seems like we are dealing with a lot of acronyms when it comes to education, but it is essential that we understand the value and meaning of each of the letters in each term.

- *ASD*: Standing for *autism spectrum disorder*, this refers to people who have autism, an ND condition that affects communication and social interactions. The key word here is 'spectrum', reminding us that the challenges and needs that each person with autism has may greatly differ; for example, some people with ASD may be able to form strong friendships and hold entertaining conversations, while some individuals may have ASD comorbid with selective mutism, a rare anxiety disorder where they are consistently unable to speak in social situations (Steffenberg et al., 2018).

- *ADHD*: *Attention deficit hyperactivity disorder* is a condition that affects a person's impulsivity, self-control and attention due to medical differences in the activity of their brain. The symptoms of this condition can be sorted into three groups: inattentiveness, hyperactivity and impulsiveness (NHS, 2021), three behaviours that we can already see may jar with many conventional and traditional styles of teaching where children are expected to sit still and focus on the work in front of them without disrupting their peers. Learners with ADHD can find it hard to follow long instructions and may need these broken down into shorter, simpler steps; multitasking and organisation can also be difficult and result in frustration for the learner.

Although all children present differently, we may see some common behaviours in the classroom:

- difficulty in regulating emotions;
- difficulty in controlling behaviour;
- difficulty in maintaining friendships or making attachments.

ND learners may also find challenges in executive functioning when it comes to organisation, starting work, or finishing work in time (Ozturk and Kızılkan, 2024).

Although all children have their own needs and strengths and weaknesses, it is important to remember that unsupported needs can lead to spiralling behaviours, which is represented in the numbers of school exclusions we see happening, a key precursor for poor outcomes (Chapman, 2023). The difficulty in diagnosing some ND conditions at a young age can come through behaviours that mirror in both NT and ND children, such as lots of energy or short attention span, as well as difficulties in verbalising how they are feeling (ibid.).

Consider how we can support all learners through choices and agency in their learning, through some strategies such as:

- choice over which activity to do;
- choice over how to present their response to a task (i.e. visual, written, or musical);
- agency over where and how to sit. Would they prefer to sit alone or with a partner or in a group? On a chair or a beanbag?

Some of these ideas may seem outside the box, but this is because often our education system defaults to a strict, outdated idea that uniform, systematic ways are the only ways; the exact ideal that neurodiversity 'diverses' from.

SUPPORTING ND LEARNERS: THE VALUE OF PLAY

Often in the literature on ND in the classroom, we see a focus on the negative behaviours and challenges that ND children may face, but it is essential to remember that there are also strengths that can be found through ND conditions:

- many children may have a hyperfocus when it comes to something they are very interested in or passionate about;
- many children with ND conditions can find creative solutions to problems and think outside the box when it comes to tasks.

Some ways that we can support ND learners include, but are not limited to, strategies such as employing visual aids, mind mapping, hands-on activities, opportunities for movement and humanities and arts (Ozturk and Kızılkan, 2024).

It is important to highlight that employing a creative pedagogy can benefit all learners, not just those who are ND, as it offers opportunities for problem solving and self-expression. Personalised learning is key for all children; however, it is not always easy or achievable when you have a busy class of 30 children with differing needs on wide spectrums. Supporting ND children through play may help counter this issue; offering opportunities from storytelling and drama can help role model social interactions and build connections (Hope Currin, 2022).

LINK TO CLASSROOM PRACTICE: CREATING A NEURO-INCLUSIVE BOOK CORNER

Take time to think about the books you have in your classroom; are the protagonists neurodiverse or neurotypical? Take time to search out some books that have ND characters to provide relatable materials for your ND students.

Did you know that BookTrust help compile lists of books relatable to certain topics or conditions?

Here are two useful booklists from BookTrust that can help you identify ND inclusive books:

- *Autism, BookTrust*: This booklist aims to provide a range of children's and teen books that feature characters who are autistic, or who have autistic spectrum conditions. www.booktrust.org.uk/booklists/a/autism/

(Continued)

- *ADHD, BookTrust:* Books are a way to provide glimpses into other people's experiences. This booklist is a range of excellent children's and teen books that feature characters with ADHD. Every child will enjoy reading them. www.booktrust.org.uk/booklists/a/adhd/

The use of children's books is also a well-recognised way to help facilitate valuable conversations with children on a range of issues. When it comes to the use of books to support neurodiversity, for adolescents identifying as ND, opportunities to see their experiences reflected in the books they read could have powerful effects on their sense of belonging and self-worth (Webber et al., 2024). For NT readers, learning about the experiences of their ND peers through accurate representation in fiction could help to promote understanding and attitudes of acceptance (ibid.).

COGNITIVE LOAD AND ONLINE LEARNING

Interestingly, we also see links between neurodiversity and successful online learning.

As mentioned earlier in this chapter, some ND learners, especially those with ASD, may find social situations difficult to read and engage with, thus we must question how supportive this environment can be, when moving to online learning – and reducing the physical social aspect (Le Cunff et al., 2024).

Of course, online learning is not always suitable when we are talking about children attending a mainstream setting, for example, but bearing in mind *cognitive load* can be valuable. Cognitive load refers to the amount of information our working memory can process at any given time. When setting instructions for your class or creating PowerPoint™ slides for a lesson, always think of the cognitive load and consider how you can lighten it through shortening sentences and keeping information as concise as possible.

In the second contribution in this chapter, Gemma Clark offers a reflection on supporting learners with dyslexia, complete with some tips to try in the classroom.

CONTRIBUTION: SUPPORTING CHILDREN WITH DYSLEXIA

BY GEMMA CLARK – PRIMARY SCHOOL TEACHER

As a teacher, neurodiversity is close to my heart. I was a child who went all through school and further education without my dyslexia ever being picked up. I vividly remember frequently being in trouble for 'refusing to learn' my times tables despite constantly trying to memorise them, often putting in late nights only to find I had no retention the following morning. I could read something aloud very fluently, but not have taken in the meaning. At secondary school, I struggled to focus when a classroom was noisy and often asked if I could sit outside the class and work. At university, I found I could concentrate in the nice, quiet library, but often had to read my psychology journal articles many times before thoroughly comprehending them. Ironically, it was a chance conversation with another dyslexic person which led to me being diagnosed with dyslexia while I was a student teacher. I was very lucky to be on a placement with a teacher who understood dyslexia very well and explained to me that dyslexia can be letters moving on a page, but it can also be problems with short-term memory, needing more processing time, difficulty with noise, difficulty memorising times tables (!) and a likelihood of having some other forms of neurodiversity. Even my lifelong terrible sense of direction and tendency to get lost without GPS navigation is due to my dyslexia.

The more I learnt about dyslexia, the more I understood myself and, importantly, the more I understood the children I was working with. I could see frustrations similar to my own showing up in the pupils I taught and found that I can usually tell if a child is dyslexic very quickly, especially if it is considered 'mild', as I recognise the intense effort, tiredness and overcompensation children put into appearing to keep up with their peers. If you suspect a child has some form of neurodiversity, it is always worth investigating. And, unfortunately, you may have to strongly advocate for children. I have many times heard professionals say diagnosis is not important if a child is 'coping'… I was coping on the outside and struggling on the inside.

I have now been teaching for many years, and something I find very important is that children should be allowed to know when they are neurodiverse, even though many people still believe that a 'label' is damaging. I strongly believe that the opposite is true. A neurodiverse child is usually very aware that they are different, but they do not understand why and think there is something 'wrong' with them or that they are not intelligent. To use dyslexia as an example, it is often very empowering for a child to learn about dyslexia. Once they understand that it is a neurological difference, that their brain functions in a way that is simply different, and that it is not related to intelligence, it can be a relief. While I do like to highlight to

(Continued)

young people that neurodiversity can come with different gifts and skill sets, I have lately come to the conclusion that it is best to steer clear of the 'superpower' narrative as that can give a child unrealistic expectations and minimise their struggles.

Another thing to understand about dyslexia is that girls are underdiagnosed. The reasons for this are complicated. For example, girls are socialised more to want to please and be compliant, which can mask symptoms as their frustrations may not always be evident by dysregulated behaviour (although, on reflection, my mum remembers my tantrums at home after a day of frustration at school).

Here are some things I would advise to help dyslexic children:

- don't overload dyslexic children with extra work. Dyslexic people get tired as our brains have to work harder. They will still be dyslexic, and they will be overtired;
- do not assume dyslexic children hate reading. I loved reading as a child (it just took me longer and I needed more quiet). A love of books does not rule out dyslexia;
- make children aware of dyslexic and neurodiverse role models (Richard Branson is a fantastic example, but try to find a diverse range);
- like the workplace, simple adjustments can make a big difference – for example, an expectation to produce less writing, more time given, less copying from a board, spelling aids;
- utilise technology; allowing children to type their work etc. is not making them reliant on technology (technology is not going anywhere), you are giving them coping strategies. However, bear in mind that sometimes children hate to be different, so be guided by them. They may be more comfortable with less noticeable adjustments;
- be aware that there can be a lot of overlap with neurodiversity. Remain curious about other conditions the child may have. The more a teacher understands a child (and the more a child understands themselves), the better;
- don't give dyslexic children (or adults) too many instructions to follow at one time;

- ask your school to find dyslexia-friendly books that are age-appropriate. Dyslexic children often feel embarrassed using reading material that is aimed at younger children. Audiobooks can also be valuable;
- it is a common misconception that coloured paper and overlays have been 'debunked'. This is not the case; it is more that not all dyslexic people suffer visual stress. It is worth checking if these are helpful for a child by simply letting them try and seeing what (if any) colours help relieve the visual stress;
- download and use dyslexia-friendly fonts. Even increased spacing and sizing can make a difference.

My most important piece of advice would be to listen to the child and work in partnership with them to discover what helps them manage their dyslexic symptoms.

LINK TO CLASSROOM PRACTICE: THANK YOU LETTER TO YOURSELF

Children write a thank you letter to themselves to appreciate their strengths and qualities that they are proud of. Asking pupils to write a letter to themselves encourages reflection and self-acceptance. Positive self-talk can help us develop confidence in who we are.

FUTURE RESEARCH INTO NEURODIVERSITY IN EDUCATION

As we mentioned at the very start of this chapter, the main way to support inclusion for ND learners (and educators!) is through having a more affirming approach to our awareness of ND conditions and needs.

There is a growing need for research to challenge misconceptions about neurodiversity in education. By interrogating the prevailing societal constructs underpinning the notion of 'normalcy', future research should deliver both conceptual and pedagogical tools to facilitate enhanced understanding of the barriers to inclusive educational practice within school contexts (Cook, 2024).

SUMMARY

- The term 'neurodivergent' (ND) is given to someone whose neural pathways work in a different way to someone classed as neurotypical (NT). The real strength of neurodiversity is that it *values differences* between people and accepts and supports unmet needs without judgement or normalisation. However, because neurodiversity is not a medical diagnosis, there is not one definitive list of conditions that are included under this umbrella term.
- Teachers may face challenges in providing inclusive education due to external pressures and regulatory frameworks. Additionally, attitudes and misconceptions about neurodiversity can further impede inclusive education and prevent the adaptation of teaching methods to cater to diverse student needs.
- Neurodiversity is a natural and valuable form of human diversity, but current educational practices often focus on diagnosis and conformity rather than embracing differences in thinking and learning. Teacher education programmes should enable a broader understanding of neurodiversity and inclusion principles, challenging the myth of the 'normal' child and preparing all teachers to respond to neurodiverse learners effectively.

7

GENDER IDENTITY AND SEXUAL ORIENTATION

INTRODUCTION

What is gender? This chapter considers inclusivity in the classroom through dissolving gender stereotypes in your class and sharing literature and activities to normalise diversity in gender and sexual orientation.

DEFINING GENDER

Gender is a complex social construct that can have a significant effect on a child's development (Ruble and Martin, 1998). Even as soon as a child is born, there are societal cues about their gender role, such as pink or blue baby-grows, or certain toys attributed to societally accepted 'girls' toys' such as a doll, or 'boys' toys' such as a dinosaur or car. Even at school, we see rules such as uniform policy, where in some settings, girls must wear skirts or dresses and not trousers (although some schools now allow girls to wear trousers as part of their uniform).

In recent years, there has been increased awareness and acceptance of gender diversity, leading to more fluid and inclusive understandings of gender (ibid.).

REFLECTIVE QUESTION 7.1

How do you define and understand the term 'gender'?

Which gender stereotypical activities or roles do you think children may fall into?

LINK TO CLASSROOM PRACTICE: WHO AM I?

This fun classroom game helps peers to get to know each other but also gives children a chance to be proud of who they are.

Ask children to write down a list of their five favourite things on a postcard or piece of paper and put their name on it.

You could give category prompts, such as favourite food, sport, singer, song, animal etc., or let the children just write five favourite things.

Collect the papers and then read them out anonymously and see if the class can guess which paper belongs to which child in the class.

This also teaches we are free to enjoy things that we like and should not be bound by societal gender norms.

To help understand the current landscape when it comes to gender diversity and sexual orientation, this chapter offers a guest contribution from Marie Greenhalgh.

CONTRIBUTION: UNDERSTANDING GENDER DIVERSITY AND SEXUAL ORIENTATION

BY MARIE GREENHALGH NPQH (SHE/HER) – INNOVATION AND DEVELOPMENT DIRECTOR (SOCIAL IMPACT), INCLUSION EDUCATION

Understanding gender diversity and sexual orientation is essential for primary-aged children as it lays the foundation for a more inclusive and accepting society. Research below highlights that children in the later primary years (ages nine to 11) begin to grasp basic concepts related to gender and sexual orientation. It also shows that children, even at a young age, are aware of and can understand concepts related to gender diversity and sexual orientation. For instance, many primary-aged children can comprehend that families can look different from their own, such as having two dads or two mums. Studies and educational reports have highlighted several key points.

A 2020 study by the UK charity Stonewall found that 45 per cent of primary school teachers had addressed LGBT+ issues in their classrooms, suggesting that many children are introduced to these topics early on (Stonewall, 2023). Additionally, 30 per cent of primary-aged children have heard of or know someone who has a family structure that includes same-sex parents.

Distressingly, research commissioned by Stonewall and YouGov showed that 70 per cent of primary school teachers heard expressions like 'that's so gay'. Almost half of them said that children in their school had experienced homophobic bullying (Stonewall, 2023).

Using negative language to describe LGBTQ+ identities sends a harmful message to children, suggesting these identities are bad. For the estimated 20,000 children in the UK being raised by LGBTQ+ parents or carers, this can lead to feelings of their family being viewed negatively, and fear and worry about this. Therefore, addressing and eliminating homophobic, biphobic and transphobic language should be a top priority for all primary schools.

From a young age, children can display signs of gender dysphoria, which may manifest as discomfort with the gender they were assigned at birth. This can present itself in various ways, often becoming more apparent as children grow and develop a stronger sense of their gender identity. Children may express a strong desire to be of a different gender or insist that they are, in fact, a different gender than the one assigned at birth. For example, a child assigned male at birth might consistently express that they are a girl and prefer being addressed with female pronouns. Many children show a strong preference for clothes, toys and activities typically associated with the opposite gender. For instance, a child assigned female at birth may prefer wearing 'boys' clothes', playing with trucks and engaging in traditionally male-associated activities.

Some children exhibit distress over their physical characteristics, or the societal expectations placed on their gender. This could manifest as discomfort with their body, particularly as they approach puberty and secondary sexual characteristics begin to develop. Children with gender dysphoria might reject traditional gender roles and stereotypes. They might feel uncomfortable or distressed when expected to conform to gender norms, such as participating in gender-segregated activities or being referred to by their birth-assigned gender.

Support from educators and safe environments is crucial in helping children navigate these feelings. The NSPCC reports that many children seek guidance and express anxieties about their gender identity, underscoring

(Continued)

the need for accessible support services and informed discussions in schools (NSPCC, 2021).

The importance of well-structured teaching on these subjects cannot be overstated. When schools proactively educate about gender diversity and sexual orientation, they often see reduced instances of bullying and improved mental wellbeing among pupils. Conversely, a lack of education can lead to misinformation and social stigma, which can harm children's mental health and social development (Jones, 2021).

Primary-aged children learn about gender roles and stereotypes through various educational activities, such as discussions about famous figures, societal roles and personal experiences. This education helps challenge traditional gender norms and fosters an environment where all children feel valued and understood. Exposure to positive representations of diverse gender identities and sexual orientations in media also helps children understand and accept diversity. TV shows featuring characters with diverse gender identities and sexual orientations provide relatable role models for children. Celebrities who openly discuss their gender identity or sexual orientation can serve as powerful role models. Their stories can help normalise these topics and provide children with positive examples of diverse identities.

Overall, the key to fostering understanding and acceptance of gender diversity and sexual orientation among primary-aged children lies in comprehensive, age-appropriate education and supportive school environments. This approach not only enriches their knowledge, but also cultivates empathy and respect for diversity from a young age.

REFLECTIVE QUESTION 7.2

How can we help normalise different sexual orientations through conversations in the primary school?

LINK TO CLASSROOM PRACTICE: LGBTQ+ INSPIRATIONAL PEOPLE

Put children in pairs and ask them to research an inspirational LGBTQ+ person and their career. You could either give each pair the name of a person, such as classic figures like James Baldwin and Harvey Milk and pop culture personalities like RuPaul and Elliott Page or let them find their own person online. They could make a PowerPoint™, create a poster, or write a poem about their chosen person to share with the class. We can use events such as Pride Month to celebrate diversity in our schools; Pride in the UK is celebrated each June, and we also celebrate LGBTQ+ History Month in February.

SUMMARY

- Gender is a complex social construct that significantly influences children's development.
- From birth, children are exposed to societal cues about gender roles and expectations.
- Researching LGBTQ+ activists and public figures can help provide positive role models.
- Pride Month and LGBTQ+ History Month are helpful in celebrating diversity in our schools.
- The key to fostering understanding and acceptance of gender diversity and sexual orientation among primary-aged children lies in comprehensive, age-appropriate education and supportive school environments.

8

CHILDREN AND AUTHORITY

INTRODUCTION

This chapter considers the relationship between child and adult and gives an overview of several psychological theories that can help us better understand this relationship. It also looks at oppositional defiant disorder (ODD) and conduct disorder in children and considers how to work with children who may present with these disorders.

AUTHORITY AND AGENCY

If we accept a definition of 'agency' as autonomous entities or agents acting or capable of acting by themselves (Toivo, 2023) it can help us consider how much agency children and young people have in their lives. In Chapter 1 of this book, we reflected on how childhood and the position of the child has changed over time, and thus it is understandable that child agency has also changed over time.

REFLECTIVE QUESTION 8.1

What agency should children and young people have, and in what situations?

How can we provide agency in the classroom?

PSYCHOLOGY THEORIES AROUND CHILDREN AND AUTHORITY

Understanding how children perceive and interact with authority figures is a complex area of study in psychology. Several theories provide insights into this relationship, and the key principle of each along with relevance in line with our pedagogy are shared below.

1. *Social learning theory*

   Key principle: Children learn by observing and imitating the behaviour of others, including authority figures.
   Relevance: If children see authority figures behaving in a positive, respectful manner, they are more likely to adopt similar behaviours. Conversely, negative or abusive behaviours can lead to negative attitudes towards authority.

2. *Attachment theory*

   Key principle: The quality of a child's attachment to primary caregivers (often parents) can influence their relationships with other authority figures.
   Relevance: Securely attached children may be more likely to trust and respect authority figures, while insecurely attached children may have difficulty forming positive relationships.

3. *Cognitive development theory*

   Key principle: Children's understanding of authority changes as they develop cognitively.
   Relevance: Younger children may view authority figures as infallible, while older children may begin to question authority and develop their own moral judgements.

4. *Power theory*

   Key principle: People's relationships with authority figures are influenced by their perceptions of power.
   Relevance: Children may be more likely to obey authority figures who they perceive as having greater power or authority.

5. *Social identity theory*

   Key principle: People's sense of self is influenced by their group memberships.
   Relevance: Children may be more likely to identify with and obey authority figures who belong to the same group as them (e.g. school, community).

6. *Authoritarian parenting*

   Key principle: A parenting style characterised by strict rules, punishment and a lack of warmth.

Relevance: Children raised by authoritarian parents may be more likely to have difficulty with authority figures, as they may associate authority with punishment and control.

These theories provide a framework for understanding children's relationships with authority figures. However, individual experiences and factors such as culture, socio-economic status and personal temperament can also influence these relationships.

REFLECTIVE QUESTION 8.2

What are your views on rewards and sanctions in the classroom; are there any you particularly like or disagree with?

Think back to any experiences you may have of going to school yourself when you were younger: how was authority exercised by teachers and the headteacher?

Did you agree with the behaviour management systems and style you experienced?

A powerful part of helping develop a balance of respect and understanding with your class is getting to know them and what makes them feel happy or frustrated.

LINK TO CLASSROOM PRACTICE: WHAT FILLS MY CUP?

Give each student a cup template printed on a piece of paper (or they could draw their own cup).

Ask them to think about what makes them happy and 'fills their cup', and then to draw or write ideas inside the cup template.

Then ask the students to think about what upsets them or makes them angry and draw or write these items around the outside of the cup.

Take time to talk to each student about their cup to help understand things that may upset them and also how to help them self-regulate in a time of frustration.

OPPOSITIONAL DEFIANT DISORDER

Oppositional defiant disorder (ODD) is a disruptive behaviour disorder involving an ongoing pattern of angry/irritable mood, argumentative/defiant behaviour and vindictiveness.

Onset is typically before eight years of age, although ODD can be diagnosed in both children and adults (Hawes et al., 2023). Sandra Shamu offers an overview of ODD in the following contribution.

CONTRIBUTION: UNDERSTANDING ODD

BY SANDRA SHAM – LECTURER IN PSYCHOLOGY, LONDON

The relationship between children and authority is fundamental in their development as this shapes and can have an impact on their understanding of the societal norms and how they interact with others. Authority figures play a huge role shaping and creating boundaries for the child to enable them to function well in society. According to Piaget (1977), young children often have a strong view on adults as the authority figure due to their age, size and the perceived power they hold. However, further research evidence has suggested that children view the legitimacy of authority based on the social context as well as the type of command being given. Children with behavioural disorders find it difficult to deal with authority which can lead them to being uncooperative and hostile to peers, parents, teachers and any other authority figures.

To meet the *Diagnostic and Statistical Manual of Mental Disorders* (5th edn, DSM-5; APA, 2013) diagnostic criteria for ODD, the child must have at least four symptoms of angry/irritable mood, argumentative/defiant behaviour, or vindictiveness. Examples of this include: often losing temper, being easily annoyed, often arguing or refusing to listen to authority, carrying out revenge-seeking behaviour, questioning rules and refusing to follow rules. For a diagnosis to be given, these symptoms must be present for at least six months and have a negative impact on social, educational, or occupational functioning.

Children with ODD have significantly difficult relationships with their parents, teachers and peers, as well as having high rates of coexisting conditions such as ADHD and mood disorders. Defiance of parents, teachers and other authoritative figures results in constant arguing, temper tantrums and rule-breaking with the intention to frustrate authority.

In a school setting this authority figure is usually mainly their teacher, with whom the child has more contact. ODD means having issues with authority

(Continued)

figures by its nature, therefore, as a teacher, being confrontational towards the student with this behavioural disorder leads to a power struggle. This can be very disruptive for both the teacher and other students in the classroom.

In order to effectively manage behaviour of children with ODD, teachers must therefore:

- shift the focus from negative behaviour and acknowledge and reward positive behaviours;
- develop a good relationship with parents/guardians and send praise reports home more often;
- create opportunities for the student to share their ideas/stories in class;
- praise positive behaviours both publicly and privately;
- identify their triggers and aim to shift their focus before they have a full-blown outburst;
- help students learn to identify their own triggers, essentially helping them to help themselves;
- create a safe space where they can reset, this could be an area in the classroom with stress relief tools, or a simple walk outside;
- not react with anger, this can make the situation worse or encourage them to continue with their bad behaviour;
- clearly communicate expectations and boundaries.

Empathy is key in fostering a trusting relationship and is important for authority figures to set clear, firm boundaries while avoiding power struggles. Behaviour management is reportedly one of the biggest stressors for teaching, and working with students displaying characteristics of ODD can turn it into an even bigger challenge. It is therefore imperative that those working with such children are provided with adequate training, guidance and emotional support to foster a good working relationship for both the teacher and student.

LINK TO CLASSROOM PRACTICE: TWO TRUTHS AND A LIE

Students share three statements about themselves, two of which are true and one false.

The other students guess which one is the lie.

As the teacher, you may want to begin by modelling three statements.

This game can be insightful as the thing picked as the 'lie' can often help you learn more about the student's perceptions of things.

CONDUCT DISORDER: A BEHAVIOURAL DISORDER

Conduct disorder is a behavioural disorder characterised by persistent patterns of aggressive, destructive and rule-breaking behaviour that often leads to significant distress or impairment. Children and adolescents with conduct disorder may engage in various problematic behaviours, including:

- *aggression*: physical aggression towards others, property damage and bullying;
- *destruction*: deliberately setting fires, damaging property, or stealing;
- *rule-breaking*: lying, truancy, running away from home and violating curfew;
- *defiance*: disobeying rules, arguing with adults and being irritable.

Symptoms of conduct disorder can vary in severity, with some individuals exhibiting mild symptoms and others engaging in more serious criminal acts. The disorder can also be a precursor to more severe problems, such as antisocial personality disorder in adulthood.

Treatment for conduct disorder often involves a combination of therapies, including:

- *cognitive-behavioural therapy*: helping individuals identify and change negative thought patterns and behaviours;
- *family therapy*: addressing family dynamics and improving communication;
- *medication*: in some cases, medication may be used to treat underlying conditions such as ADHD or depression.

Earlier in this book, we considered the valuable partnership between home and school. If you are concerned about a child or adolescent's behaviour, it is important to ensure you are communicating with parents and carers and involving school support staff such as the SENCO as necessary. Early intervention can help prevent the development of more serious problems.

LINK TO CLASSROOM PRACTICE: HUMAN BINGO

Create a bingo card with different characteristics or interests.

Students move around the room to find classmates who match the descriptions on their card.

This is a good way for peers to talk to others in the class they may not normally talk to.

SUMMARY

- Individual experiences and factors such as culture, socio-economic status and personal temperament can influence the relationship a child has with adults.
- Children raised by authoritarian parents may be more likely to have difficulty with authority figures, as they may associate authority with punishment and control.
- Securely attached children may be more likely to trust and respect authority figures, while insecurely attached children may have difficulty forming positive relationships.
- Empathy is key in fostering a trusting relationship; it is important for authority figures to set clear, firm boundaries while avoiding power struggles. If children see authority figures behaving in a positive, respectful manner, they are more likely to adopt similar behaviours.

9

CHILDREN AND SEND

INTRODUCTION

This chapter is all about special educational needs and disabilities (SEND). A broad discussion is held around how we can support children with a range of SEND in our classrooms, and the importance of communication with parents and carers. SEND and the full complexities of supporting children and parents of children with SEND cannot be covered in one chapter; however, the aim is to give an insight into the wider picture of special needs, exploring some key information.

DEFINING SEND

Special educational needs (SEN) can be defined as a broad range of difficulties that can affect a child's learning, development, or behaviour. These needs may be present at birth or develop later in life and can vary in severity. It's important to note that 'SEN' is a broad term and can encompass a wide range of conditions. The specific needs of each child will vary, and what constitutes SEN can also differ depending on the educational system and cultural context. Some common examples of SEN include:

- *learning difficulties*: these can affect reading, writing, or maths skills;
- *communication and language difficulties*: these can impact a child's ability to understand or express themselves;
- *social, emotional and mental health difficulties*: these can affect a child's behaviour, relationships, or self-esteem;
- *physical and sensory impairments*: these can include visual, hearing, or physical disabilities.

REFLECTIVE QUESTION 9.1

When did SEN first become recognised in the educational landscape?

The report of the Warnock Committee (Warnock, 1978) was a landmark event for the education of children and young people with SEN. The Committee produced a wide-ranging examination of the whole SEN system of the time and, taking into account recent research and existing progressive practice, produced a report that formed the basis for substantial conceptual, administrative and practice changes (Lindsay et al., 2020). Part of the focus was on parental power and partnership; however, decades later there is still disparity in how parents are supported (ibid.).

We are also seeing rising awareness of 'invisible disabilities' in society. Invisible disabilities frequently relate to learning and psychiatric challenges not initially or overtly visible (Carlisle, 2022), including neurodivergent conditions such as dyslexia, ADHD and ASD, discussed in more detail in Chapter 6 on neurodiversity.

THE CHALLENGE OF INCLUSION FOR ALL

In today's educational climate, the responsibility for teaching students with special needs no longer lies exclusively with special education (SPED) teachers (Byrd and Alexander, 2020)

REFLECTIVE QUESTION 9.2

How can we ensure inclusion for all in mainstream classrooms; is this even possible or achievable?

Full inclusion in education for children with SEND is a complex and controversial issue. While international pressure promotes it, national concerns about educational standards raise questions about its feasibility.

The Salamanca Statement (CSIE, 1994) outlined the aspirational goal of full inclusion, but its implementation has faced challenges. Full inclusion requires schools to address a wide range of SEND. Current legislation acknowledges this, but doesn't specify how teachers should manage diverse needs or provide necessary support. There is the need for governments, teachers and schools to recognise the full spectrum of SEND and the implications for leadership, staffing and resources. While the UNCRPD promotes full inclusion, it doesn't account for the specialist knowledge and skills teachers need to effectively support all children (Gordon-Gould and Hornby, 2023).

LINK TO CLASSROOM PRACTICE: ANTI-BULLYING ACTIVITY

Put the class into small groups (approximately three to four students per group) and give them fictional bullying activities, either printed on paper or written on the board. The scenarios you create will vary depending on your class's age and emotional understanding, but may include fictional stories such as:

- a new girl joins the class; she has a large birthmark on her face and you overhear some children making fun of her in the playground behind her back. What would you do?
- you are in an online chat group; someone says something unkind about a member of your class who is in a wheelchair. What would you do?

After giving the groups time to discuss each scenario, ask each group to share their ideas with the class.

CONTRIBUTION: INCLUSION FOR EVERY CHILD

BY JESSICA WYTHE – LECTURER IN EARLY CHILDHOOD STUDIES AND EDUCATION STUDIES AT BIRMINGHAM CITY UNIVERSITY

As a former SEND practitioner in various Early Years education settings, mainstream primary schools and specialist provision settings turned lecturer in Early Childhood Studies and Education Studies, my journey has evolved from directly supporting children with diverse needs to now shaping the future educators of our generation. In this pivotal role, I am dedicated to equipping aspiring teachers with the knowledge, skills and mindset necessary to foster inclusive classrooms and promote educational equity.

Central to my pedagogical approach is the belief that every child, regardless of their background or abilities, deserves access to high quality education in an environment that values diversity and celebrates individual strengths. With this vision in mind, I am committed to instilling in future educators a deep understanding of inclusion and equity and providing them with practical strategies

(Continued)

to translate these principles into action. In my lectures and seminars, I emphasise the profound impact that small changes by the teacher can have for children with SEND.

Implementing visual timetables has proven invaluable in nurturing independence and autonomy among children with SEND, empowering them to navigate classroom routines with confidence and self-reliance. By providing a clear visual representation of daily activities, these timetables enhance their awareness and understanding of classroom expectations, fostering a sense of control and predictability that helps to alleviate anxiety and promote a positive learning environment.

Additionally, incorporating multisensory teaching methods, such as hands-on activities and auditory cues, ensures that instruction is accessible to all learners, accommodates diverse learning styles and promotes active engagement with the curriculum. Finally, regular communication with parents and support staff is crucial in ensuring that children's individual needs with SEND are met effectively. By maintaining open communication channels, educators can collaborate with families and specialists to develop personalised strategies and interventions that support academic and social success in school and beyond. In doing so, they empower children with SEND to thrive and reach their full potential, laying the foundation for lifelong learning and achievement.

One key aspect of my teaching in higher education is integrating and implementing research-informed approaches to inclusive education. By introducing students to current literature and evidence-based practices, I empower them to recognise the value of small changes and understand how these adjustments can make a profound difference for children with SEND. Through critical reflection and case studies, future educators learn to identify barriers to learning and develop targeted strategies to address them effectively. I also emphasise the importance of creating supportive and inclusive learning environments that value and respect the unique experiences and identities of all students. My students are encouraged to actively engage with issues of social justice, diversity and inclusion, both within and beyond the classroom. By fostering a culture of empathy, collaboration and lifelong learning, I aim to inspire them to become advocates for educational equity in their future careers.

My students are always encouraged to consider the perspectives of children with SEND and recognise the significance of their role in facilitating positive learning experiences. By fostering empathy and understanding, future educators learn to appreciate each child's unique challenges and strengths, empowering them to create inclusive learning environments where every student can thrive. Ultimately, implementing small changes with intentionality and compassion allows teachers and educators to create safe spaces within their classrooms where every child feels seen, heard and valued. These intentional adjustments, whether it's offering flexible seating options, incorporating visual supports, or fostering peer support systems, have a ripple effect that extends far beyond the classroom walls. They not only enhance academic learning, but also promote social–emotional development and contribute to the overall wellbeing of children with SEND. Through their commitment to inclusive practice and continuous reflection, educators play a pivotal role in shaping the experiences and outcomes of children with SEND, laying the foundation for a more equitable and inclusive society.

In preparing the future educators of our generation, I am mindful of the transformative impact they can have on the lives of countless children and families. By equipping my students with the knowledge, skills and passion to promote inclusion and equity, I am confident that they will go on to create classrooms where every child feels valued, supported and empowered to reach their full potential. Together, we can work towards a future where education is truly inclusive, equitable and transformative for all.

LINK TO CLASSROOM PRACTICE: DOUBLE DRAWINGS!

The aim of this game is to show we all interpret things differently.

Put students into groups of three. In each group, one person will be the speaker and two will be the artists. If you have an equal number, you can have more artists in a group, but only one speaker. Give the speaker an object in secret (or they could pick one from a bag or box etc.). Don't let the artists see the item.

Give the artists paper and something to draw with. The speaker has 60 seconds (or longer if you feel it's needed) to describe the item to the artists so that they can draw it. The speaker must not say what the item is – just describe it.

When time is up, ask artists to show their drawings. Use this as a stimulus to discuss how we all interpret things differently.

In the following contribution, Shazad Ali encourages us to consider how we need to take a holistic approach to supporting students, especially those students who cannot engage in mainstream settings.

CONTRIBUTION: INTERNAL ALTERNATIVE EDUCATIONAL PROVISIONS (AEPS): A HOLISTIC APPROACH TO SUPPORTING STUDENTS WITH SPECIAL NEEDS

BY SHAZAD ALI – ALTERNATIVE EDUCATION PROVISIONS MANAGER

In today's educational landscape, many students face challenges that mainstream schools are not equipped to address fully. This is where internal AEPs come into play. Designed to support students with special needs who struggle in traditional settings, AEPs provide a nurturing environment that addresses behavioural, emotional and learning barriers. This piece of work looks at the key components critical to the success of AEPs: building relationships, identifying needs, tailoring the curriculum and facilitating reintegration, with a focus on how school leaders can effectively implement these strategies.

1. *Building relationships*

At the heart of successful AEPs is the establishment of strong, trusting relationships between staff and students. Drawing on Maslow's hierarchy of needs, it is clear that students thrive when their basic needs for safety, belonging and love are met. Dr James Comer's insight, 'no significant learning can occur without a significant relationship' (1995), highlights the importance of these connections.

In AEPs, where students often carry emotional baggage from past educational experiences, staff must act as mentors and allies. Training in trauma-informed practices is crucial, enabling educators to look beyond surface behaviours and understand the underlying issues students may be expressing. By responding with empathy and support, educators create a safe space conducive to learning.

2. *Finding and identifying needs*

Students in AEPs often have unmet needs that hinder their success in mainstream education. These might include low self-esteem, difficulty with large class sizes, or unaddressed trauma. Early identification of these needs is essential.

Baseline assessments are vital tools in this process. Comprehensive evaluations, including input from the SEN team, help identify learning difficulties and provide up-to-date data on academic abilities. Beyond academics, understanding a student's psychological and emotional needs is crucial. This holistic approach ensures that students receive the accommodations necessary for success, such as access arrangements for exams.

3. *Curriculum adaptation*

The curriculum in an AEP must be tailored to meet each student's unique needs, aiming to remove learning barriers and prepare them for reintegration into mainstream education. While following the same mainstream scheme of work, adaptations may include differentiated instruction, modified assignments, or additional support.

Collaboration with mainstream teaching staff is essential to ensure alignment with the broader school curriculum. Sharing successful strategies and evidence-based practices facilitates a smoother transition for students. Linking the curriculum to students' future career aspirations can also enhance engagement, helping them see the relevance of their education to their long-term goals.

4. *Reintegration*

The ultimate goal of an AEP is to reintegrate students into mainstream education successfully. This process relies on the evidence and data collected during the student's time in the AEP.

5. *Strategic scaffolding*

Providing the right amount of support at the right time is key. As students progress, support is gradually reduced to build independence and resilience. Once reintegrated, it is crucial to share effective strategies with the whole school to ensure continued support. This collaborative approach helps maintain the progress students have made and fosters a supportive environment that encourages ongoing success.

Internal AEPs play a vital role in supporting students who struggle in mainstream education. By focusing on building strong relationships, accurately

(Continued)

identifying needs, tailoring the curriculum and carefully managing the reintegration process, AEPs help students overcome significant challenges and achieve success. The work done within these provisions is not just about addressing academic deficits; it's about rebuilding confidence, fostering resilience and empowering students to reach their full potential. School leaders are encouraged to invest in and support AEPs, recognising their transformative impact on students' lives.

REFLECTIVE QUESTION 9.3

What does parental choice look like for parents and carers of children with SEND?

In this next contribution, Charlotte Maskrey focuses on the challenges that may be faced by autistic girls in education and encourages us to consider how to support them.

CONTRIBUTION: AUTISTIC GIRLS IN EDUCATION

BY CHARLOTTE MASKREY – SEND EDUCATOR

After decades of advocacy and activism we are finally making our way towards a neuro-inclusive society. Slowly. One of the biggest barriers relating to neurodiversity I see regularly is the huge gender disparity relating to both diagnosis and identifying of autistic characteristics. For years autistics girls were seen as unicorns – rare, and therefore invisible. Our understanding of autism was based solely around how characteristics presented themselves in young boys, leaving millions of autistic girls struggling in silence. The diagnosis rates of boys to girls have begun to creep from 4:1 historically to 3:1 and now, finally, leaning closer to 2:1 as our diagnostic tools become more inclusive. But many autistic girls are still not diagnosed until adolescence or adulthood due to female autistic traits not being as commonly known and diagnostic tools being male-focused

(Loomes et al., 2017). This has left millions of young autistic girls masking every day, like swans peaceful on the surface and kicking desperately to stay afloat under the surface. The mental health struggle of autistic girls is an epidemic.

As educators it is incredibly important to understand the key traits appearing in autistic girls to help support this long-ignored group to reach diagnosis and therefore gain the support they need. One key trait that can mean autistic girls go undiagnosed for so long is camouflaging or social mimicry, imitating social behaviours and on the surface appearing comfortable or confident in social settings. However, this excessive masking leads to burnout and poor mental health. The stereotype that all autistic individuals struggle with a lack of empathy has led countless autistic girls to receive misdiagnoses. For autistic girls, empathy can be heightened, appearing incredibly emotionally sensitive and therefore being more prone to anxiety, depression, low self-esteem and increasing the likelihood of experiencing meltdowns and shutdowns from internalised distress. Many autistic girls experience overwhelming empathy, especially relating to animals or inanimate objects. Sensory sensitivities are another huge trait for autistic girls, struggling with hyposensitivity (under-sensitivity) and seeking out sensory stimuli or hypersensitivity (over-sensitivity) and therefore feeling distressed and overwhelmed by sensory stimuli. Motor skills can also be a key identifier for autistic girls; many individuals will struggle with fine motor skills such as handwriting. Another key trait of autism in girls is passionate and restrictive interests; these may go under the radar for many individuals as the interests may be seen as more 'socially acceptable' or 'gender normative'. Signs of these specific interests may be restrictive conversations limited to specific topics, a mammoth amount of depth and detail being known about the topic (many autistic girls are experts about their special interests) and using the special interest as a comfort or way to reduce anxiety. Many autistic girls will also have co-occurring conditions such as OCD, eating disorders and ADHD which can make it even trickier for them to gain a diagnosis.

To reach the goal of a neuro-inclusive society, we must make sure our inclusivity spans all genders; this starts by understanding the autistic girl experience and continues by creating an environment that nurtures and supports their authentic autistic selves.

LINK TO CLASSROOM PRACTICE: SIMILARITIES AND DIFFERENCES SIMON SAYS

This version of 'Simon says' helps children recognise similarities and differences between their peers.

Explain to the class that they will play a version of Simon says, and they need to respond to statements that apply to them. Tell the class that they must watch and listen carefully as they play the game because, at the end, each person must say one new thing they learnt about another member of the class.

Play the game of Simon says using statements such as the following examples; you can tailor them to more closely fit the conversations you are having with your class:

- if you have blue eyes, put your hands on your head;
- if you are left-handed, wave your left hand in the air;
- if you speak more than one language, rub your stomach.

After the game, ask each member of the class to say one way in which they and another of their peers is alike.

In this final contribution, Mark Watts shares an insightful reflection of supporting his son, Jack, who has Down syndrome and autism.

CONTRIBUTION: THE BENEFITS OF CALM MUSIC FOR LEARNING-DISABLED ADULTS: A HOLISTIC APPROACH

BY MARK WATTS – SENIOR LECTURER IN PUBLIC SERVICES AT REDCAR AND CLEVELAND COLLEGE

What links Fleetwood Mac's song 'Albatross' and Edvard Grieg's *Peer Gynt*?

Answer: my son Jack, a 27-year-old with Down syndrome and autism. These diverse music genres were the start of a mindfulness journey that I would recommend any person taking. These were our 'go-to' when he became overwhelmed and, over a period, I recognised that this may be something to develop at the *trigger* stage of crisis.

For learning-disabled adults, managing daily challenges often requires a multifaceted approach that nurtures both the mind and body. Calm music has emerged as a powerful tool in promoting emotional wellbeing, enhancing focus and fostering relaxation. When combined with mindful positioning and breathing techniques, it can offer a holistic way to improve the quality of life and enhance cognitive functioning.

THE POWER OF CALM MUSIC

Calm music, often characterised by soft melodies, slow tempos and gentle harmonies, has a unique ability to soothe the nervous system. Research shows that listening to calming music can reduce anxiety, lower blood pressure and even decrease levels of the stress hormone cortisol. For learning-disabled adults, who may experience heightened anxiety or sensory overload, the use of calm music can be particularly beneficial because this type of music creates an auditory environment that promotes relaxation and can help to establish a sense of safety and predictability. Playing soft instrumental music during routine activities can help reduce anxiety and create a calming atmosphere, making daily tasks more manageable. Moreover, the regular exposure to calm music can assist in regulating emotions, which is crucial for learning-disabled adults who may struggle with emotional regulation.

POSITION AND BREATHING

The physical position of the body during music listening can significantly impact its effectiveness. For instance, a seated position with the spine straight and shoulders relaxed allows for better oxygen flow and helps the body to remain calm and centred. Jack, however, prefers the prone position on his back with head on a pillow. A simple copying exercise was used to consider the role of positioning and breathing. These techniques – particularly deep, diaphragmatic breathing – are another key component. Deep breathing involves inhaling slowly through the nose, allowing the abdomen to rise and then exhaling through the mouth. This type of breathing helps to activate

(Continued)

the parasympathetic nervous system, which counteracts the body's stress response and promotes a state of relaxation.

THE PAY OFF

This is still a learning journey we are on; however, Jack is far better balanced than previously and can start these techniques on his own – a major result! Incorporating calm music into the lives of learning-disabled adults offers a holistic approach to enhancing emotional and mental wellbeing. When combined with mindful positioning, breathing techniques and, eventually, some form of meditation, calm music becomes a powerful tool for managing stress, improving focus and fostering a sense of calm. By integrating these practices into daily routines, learning-disabled adults can experience a greater quality of life, with more control over their emotions and a better ability to navigate the challenges they face.

SUMMARY

- SEN can be defined as a broad range of difficulties that can affect a child's learning, development, or behaviour.
- These needs may be present at birth or develop later in life and can vary in severity.
- It's important to note that 'SEN' is a broad term and can encompass a wide range of conditions.
- The specific needs of each child will vary, and what constitutes SEN can also differ depending on the educational system and cultural context.
- The report of the Warnock Committee (Warnock, 1978) was a landmark event for the education of children and young people with SEN, but there is still much work to be done in inclusion, support and parental choice.

10

CHILDREN WHO ARE VERY ABLE

INTRODUCTION

How can we stretch and challenge able children to ensure they stay motivated and engaged? This chapter shares some practical ideas on supporting children who may be deemed as *able* or *gifted and talented*, along with two contributions of lived experiences from practitioners.

GIFTED AND TALENTED

'Gifted and talented' is a term sometimes used to describe children who exhibit exceptional abilities or talents in one or more areas, such as:

- *intellectual abilities*: high IQ (intelligence quotient), advanced problem-solving skills and rapid learning;
- *creative abilities*: exceptional imagination, originality and artistic expression;
- *leadership abilities*: strong interpersonal skills, natural leadership qualities and the ability to motivate others;
- *specific academic talents*: exceptional abilities in subjects like mathematics, science, languages, arts, or music.

It's important to note that giftedness and talent, or being 'very able', can manifest in various ways and at different ages. Some children may show early signs of exceptional abilities, while others may develop their talents later on in life.

REFLECTIVE QUESTION 10.1

How do you perceive gifted and talented and what is the value of this label in the classroom? Is it helpful or a hindrance?

Does the description here fit your own understanding of the terms 'able' or 'gifted and talented'?

Can you think of any specific examples you've encountered?

LINK TO CLASSROOM PRACTICE: CHOICE

The main thing to stress is to give children choice in the classroom.

This can be, for example, choosing how to present their homework project.

Give them options such as to create a video, make a PowerPoint, or construct a 3D model.

Giving choice lets children showcase their talent in the way that they choose.

THE EXPERIENCE OF PARENTING GIFTED CHILDREN

Research on the daily experiences of parents raising gifted children is limited. A qualitative study by Peebles et al. (2023) interviewed 12 parents of primary-age gifted children to explore their experiences.

REFLECTIVE QUESTION 10.2

What do you think may be the challenges of being a parent or carer to a child who is very able, or gifted and talented?

On the one hand, raising gifted children shares challenges with raising average-ability children, giftedness presents unique stressors. Themes included a 'child-driven' parenting approach, social isolation and physical and emotional exhaustion (ibid.).

On the other hand, raising a gifted child presents unique challenges, with their intellectual and emotional needs requiring specific attention. Parents often feel uninformed about these needs, leading to difficulties such as limited resources, societal hostility and feelings of isolation (de Souza Fleith et al., 2024).

REFLECTIVE QUESTION 10.3

How can teachers group children in ways to support very able students?

Do you think same-ability pairing or mixed-ability pairing is better, and why?

CONTRIBUTION: THE 'CUTAWAY' APPROACH TO GROUPING: 'WHO DO I NEED HERE NOW?'

BY DR KEITH WATSON – ASSOCIATE AT THE NATIONAL ASSOCIATION FOR ABLE CHILDREN IN EDUCATION (NACE)

In recent years many new developments in teaching have been most welcome and have helped the shift towards a more research-informed profession. NACE's report, *Making Space for Able Learners. Cognitive Challenge: Principles into Practice* (Lowe and McCarthy, 2020) provides examples of strategies used for the design and management of cognitively challenging learning opportunities, including reference to Rosenshine's *Principles of Instruction* (2010) which outline many of these strategies. I was always taken by Professor Deborah Eyre's reference to 'structured tinkering' (2002): not wholesale change but building upon key principles and existing practice.

This is where *cutaway* comes in – another of the strategies identified in the NACE report, and one which I would like to encourage you to 'tinker' with in your approach to ability grouping and ensuring appropriately challenging learning for all.

WHAT IS CUTAWAY AND WHY USE IT?

The cutaway approach involves setting high-attaining students off to start their independent work earlier than the vast majority of the class, while the

(Continued)

teacher continues to provide direct instruction/modelling to the main group. In this way the high attainers can begin their independent work more quickly and can avoid being bored by the whole-class instruction which they can find too easy, even when the teacher is trying to 'teach to the top'. Once the rest of the class has begun their independent work, the teacher can then focus on the higher-attaining group to consolidate the independent work and extend them further.

There are more nuances which I will explain later, but you may wonder: how did this way of working come about?

An often-quoted figure from the National Academy of Gifted and Talented Youth (NAGTY) was that higher-attaining students may already have acquired knowledge of 40–50 per cent of their lessons before they are taught (Watson, 2005). If I am honest, this was 100 per cent in some of my old lessons! With whole-class teaching, retrieval practice tasks and modelling (all essential elements in a lesson), there are clear dangers of pupils being asked to work on things they already know well. There is the issue of what Freeman (quoted in Ofsted, 1998: 3) called the 'three-time problem' where: 'Pupils who absorb the information the first time develop a technique of mentally switching off for the second and the third, then switching on again for the next new point, involving considerable mental skill.' In a school I recently reviewed a Year 10 pupil said, 'Sometimes it's as if the PowerPoint is doing the talking and I just think, can't I get on with it now?' Why waste their time?

The idea of cutaway was consolidated when I carried out a research project involving the use of learning logs to improve teaching provision for more able learners (Watson, 2005). In this project teachers adapted their teaching based on pupil feedback. The teachers realised that, in a primary classroom, keeping the pupils too long 'on the carpet' was inappropriate and the length of time available to work at a high level was being minimised. One of the teachers reflected: 'Sometimes during shared work on the carpet, when revising work from previous lessons to check the understanding of other pupils, I feel aware of the more able children wanting to move on straight away and find it difficult to balance the needs of all the children within the Year 5 class.'

It therefore became common in lessons (though not all lessons) to cutaway pupils when they were ready to begin independent work. By using cutaway the pupils use time more effectively, develop greater independence, can move through work more quickly and carry out more extended and more challenging tasks. The method was commented upon favourably during an HMI inspection that my school received and has ever since been a mainstay of teaching at the school.

WHO, WHEN AND HOW TO CUTAWAY

So how does a teacher decide when and who to cutaway? The method is not needed in all lessons; the cutaway group should vary based upon assessment for learning (AfL), and at its best it involves pupils deciding whether they feel they need more modelling/explanation from the teacher or are ready to be cutaway. In a recent NACE blogpost on ability grouping, Dr Ann McCarthy (2021) emphasises that, in using cutaway, 'the teacher constantly assesses pupils' learning and needs and directs their learning to maximise opportunities, growth and development' and pupils 'leave and join the shared learning community'. This underlines the importance of the AfL nature of the strategy and the importance of developing learners' metacognition. It is *adaptive teaching* in action.

Sometimes the cutaway approach is decided on before a lesson by the teacher based upon previous work. In GCSE history, a basic retrieval task on the Norman invasion could be time wasted for a more able pupil who has secure knowledge, whereas being cutaway to do an independent task centred on the role of the Pope in supporting William would be more challenging and worthwhile. It comes down to key questions a teacher needs to ask themselves when speaking to the whole class. *Who do I need here now?* Who needs to retrieve this knowledge? Who needs to hear this explanation? Who needs to see this model or complete this example? If a small group of higher attainers do not need this, then why slow the pace of their learning? Why not start them either on the same work independently or more challenging work to accelerate learning?

Why not play around with this idea? Explain your thinking to the pupils and see how they respond. Sometimes, at the end of one lesson, a task for the next lesson can be explained and the pupils could start the next lesson by working on that task straight away. The 2015 *Ofsted Inspection Handbook* said, 'The expectation is that the majority of pupils will move through the programmes of study at the same pace' (p. 19), and ideally, they will. However, a few pupils will progress at a faster rate and therefore need adapted provision, so why not cut them away?

LINK TO CLASSROOM PRACTICE: CHILLI CHALLENGE

Building on the first link in this chapter, chilli challenge is a way you can offer simple activity choice to your class.

Prepare three activities of varying difficulty: the easiest is the 'mild chilli', the middle one is the 'medium chilli' and the hardest activity is the 'spicy chilli'. You could even make a 'ghost chilli' challenge for any pupils who complete the spicy chilli work!

Giving students ownership of activity allows for self-reflection and self-challenge.

This also requires monitoring and facilitation by the teacher if the student is choosing the wrong 'spice level' by guiding them which level to try.

This second contribution from Poncelet Ileleji encourages us to consider how digital tools can help pupils show their potential.

CONTRIBUTION: A GIFTED CHILD ENABLED BY EXPLORING, EXCHANGING AND EXPRESSING, AIDED BY DIGITAL TECHNOLOGIES

BY PONCELET ILELEJI – CEO, JOKKOLABS BANJUL, THE GAMBIA, EDUCATIONAL TECHNOLOGIST ENTHUSIAST

In today's massive digital-enabled world, talent and skill among children can be put down to three things: *exploring, exchanging* and *expressing*. In saying this, any child, whatever part of the world they may live in, deserves better access to educational technologies to unlock their potential to fully explore, exchange and express themselves.

The UN Sustainable Development Goal 4 (SDG 4) on quality education states we should: 'Ensure inclusive and equitable quality education and promote lifelong learning opportunities for all' (Global Campaign for Education, 2024). The UN (2022) report shows over 147 million children missed in-person instruction during the COVID pandemic; this placed a lot of pressure on families and governments to do something to bridge the gap. Unfortunately, most countries affected were those considered 'developing countries', as defined by the Organisation for Economic Cooperation and Development (OECD).

In the context of equity, all children are gifted if given the right opportunity to excel where educational opportunities and equal access to technology and the internet is possible. In Sub Saharan Africa, where Broadband access is only at 37 per cent, a lot is expected. The International Telecommunication Union (ITU) reports that, as of 2023, one third of the global population remains offline, which is worrying and only heightens disparity in outcomes (ITU, 2023). In countries like the UK, being online has facilitated children being able to develop their full learning ability aided by a participatory approach that is no longer teacher-centric. My hope is that through digital technologies we can see the true potential of a child through being able to exchange, explore and express.

In conclusion, achieving quality education according to the stated objective of the UN SDGs starts with teachers being equipped and retrained regularly to know how important digital technologies can aid a child's growth to exchange, express and explore better. We are dependent on researchers in education making digital technology resources more open for the collective good of humanity; a hard task, but doable.

LINK TO CLASSROOM PRACTICE: FIXED TIME OR WORD COUNT

Challenge pupils through setting a tight timer or word count for a task. For example, give them only one minute to write a response to a question, or prescribe the number of words to be used to make very able pupils think hard about what they write, and make every word count.

SUMMARY

- 'Gifted and talented' is a term sometimes used to describe children who exhibit exceptional abilities or talents in one or more areas. It's important to note that giftedness and talent can manifest in various ways and at different ages. Some children may show early signs of exceptional abilities, while others may develop their talents later in life.
- Children can be gifted in many areas, not just academically – for example, in leadership skills.
- We must remember that it is through the activities and resources we provide for our students that they can truly show their potential.

11

CHILDREN AND PHOBIAS

INTRODUCTION

Even as adults, we have things that we fear – for example, some people are terrified of spiders – but are these phobias or just fears? What is the difference, and can anyone truly be cured of a phobia or are they long-term? This chapter explores the research and literature on children and phobias, along with some of the more common phobias that children may experience and how to support children with phobias in the classroom.

FEAR, ANXIETY AND PHOBIAS

Common *fears* in early childhood include animals, insects, storms, heights, water, blood and the dark. These fears usually go away gradually on their own (NHS, 2023a).

Fears come from a place of anxiety; we have seen more children and young people presenting with anxiety in recent years, with disorders in the form of symptoms of anxiety occurring in 10–15 per cent of cases (Temirpulotovich, 2023).

Experiencing feelings of anxiousness is a normal human emotion. *Anxiety* refers to a state of excessive worry, a state of worry being experienced by an individual, despite no immediate threat being present, or at levels of worry that may be regarded as being disproportionate to the identified risk (Glasofer, 2021).

LINK TO CLASSROOM PRACTICE: OVERCOMING FEARS

Talk to your class about something that you are afraid of. Then talk about ways you overcome that fear.

Encourage your class to do the same – they could draw the thing they are scared of and then write ways to overcome or alleviate fears underneath.

A *phobia* is characterised by persistent fear of a specific object or situation that interferes with functioning or causes significant distress (Seligman et al., 2023). A specific phobia is an intense, enduring fear of something associated with anxiety symptoms, distress and avoidance (APA, 2013), estimated to affect 5–10 per cent of children and young people. Living with severe phobias can affect quality of life and lead to struggles with academic work and mental health problems including long-term phobia (Wright et al., 2023).

REFLECTIVE QUESTION 11.1

Are there any things you have a phobia of, or is it just a fear?

Can you remember when you were growing up, were there any things you were scared of?

So why do phobias develop? It seems there are many factors that can contribute to the manifestation of a phobia, including genetic influences, temperamental predispositions, parental psychopathology, parenting practices and individual conditioning histories (Ollendick et al., 2002). There are different categories of phobias:

- *specific phobias*, also known as simple phobias, which are the most common and focus on specific objects;
- *social phobias*, which cause extreme anxiety in social or public situations.

Individuals with social phobias report higher levels of fearfulness, loneliness and depression (Strauss and Last, 1993).

Some common phobias include:

- phobia of the dark (nyctophobia);
- phobia of the dentist or dental phobia (dentophobia, also called odontophobia);
- phobia of blood (hemophobia);
- phobia of spiders (arachnophobia);
- phobia of open spaces or being in a space without escape (agoraphobia);
- phobia of dogs (cynophobia).

LINK TO CLASSROOM PRACTICE: WHEN I'M FEELING SCARED

Explain to the class we all feel scared sometimes. We feel scared if we feel threatened or in danger, or if we are nervous about doing something we haven't done before.

Collect ways that we can help calm down when we are feeling scared and list them up on the board. Ideas may include:

- take deep breaths to feel calm again;
- say to myself 'I am scared, but I can do this';
- draw what you are scared of and then make it funny or silly – like a spider, and then give it a party hat and funny shoes;
- talk to an adult or someone I trust about what is scaring me;
- put the scary thing in perspective;
- think about the future when the scary thing may be over.

COMMON TREATMENTS FOR PHOBIAS

The most effective treatment for phobias is therapy, specifically cognitive-behavioural therapy (CBT). CBT helps you manage your thoughts, feelings and behaviours related to your fear.

Key techniques used in CBT for phobias include:

- *exposure therapy*: gradually and repeatedly exposing yourself to the feared object or situation in a safe and controlled environment;
- *cognitive restructuring*: identifying and challenging negative thoughts about the feared object or situation;
- *relaxation techniques*: learning to manage physical symptoms of anxiety, such as rapid heartbeat or sweating.

In some cases, medication may be prescribed to help manage anxiety or depression. However, therapy is generally considered the primary treatment for phobias.

USE OF VIRTUAL REALITY (VR)

Virtual reality (VR) is emerging as a promising tool for treating adult anxiety disorders. While research on VR for children lags behind, studies suggest its effectiveness for specific phobias, particularly school and spider phobias. However, VR's effectiveness may depend on addressing children's underlying fears and tailoring stimuli to their age (Bouchard, 2011).

Dental phobia is a common childhood issue that can lead to avoidance of dental care. VR therapy offers a promising solution. By immersing patients in a virtual world, VR can distract from dental procedures, reducing anxiety and pain. Studies highlight the effectiveness of VR in managing dental phobia and improving the overall dental experience for children (Rosa et al., 2023).

Dark phobia is another common childhood fear. Exposure therapy, a proven treatment for phobias, can be effectively delivered through VR games. VR games offer a safe, engaging and effective way to treat dark phobia in children. While previous VR research has focused on other childhood phobias, there's potential for tailored games to address dark fears. Designing these games requires careful consideration of children's perspectives, fears and interactive preferences. NoPhobia is a VR game designed to alleviate dark phobia in four- to six-year-old children. It incorporates insights from surveys, interviews and existing research to create a child-friendly, immersive experience that addresses specific fear triggers and offers interactive elements (Su and Yan, 2023)

Virtual reality environments (VREs) offer potential for psychological treatment and assessment such as deep breathing training for anxiety, treating internet gaming disorder and anorexia nervosa, and assessing body image in anorexia nervosa. The current literature shows promise for VREs in childhood mental health, particularly for anxiety disorders. Given their potential to improve engagement and outcomes, VREs could be a valuable addition to treatment options for young people (Blanco et al., 2023).

LINK TO CLASSROOM PRACTICE: MY TOP FIVE WORRIES

Give each student a piece of paper and ask them to draw their face in the middle.

Then ask them to draw five lines coming out from the picture and write down their top five worries. Students can then either share and discuss with a partner or share with the teaching assistant or teacher.

It could also be a useful activity to be shared with parents and carers, so they know how their child is feeling.

SUMMARY

- A phobia is characterised by persistent fear of a specific object or situation that interferes with functioning or causes significant distress.

- Living with severe phobias can affect quality of life and lead to struggles with academic work and mental health problems including long-term phobia.
- In some cases, medication may be prescribed to help manage anxiety or depression. However, therapy is generally considered the primary treatment for phobias.
- There are many factors that can contribute to the manifestation of a phobia, including genetic influences, temperamental predispositions, parental psychopathology, parenting practices and individual conditioning histories.
- VREs offer potential for psychological treatment and assessment.

12

CHILDREN AND COMMUNICATION

INTRODUCTION

In this chapter, we consider reasons that children may have difficulty communicating and discuss the nuances in communication and nonverbal communication.

This chapter also shares valuable contributions from two educators: Lauren Tickner, Primary Education Graduate, gives an important overview of Makaton™, and Mel Green, Lecturer in Education Studies, shares an insightful personal experience of parenting and supporting a nonverbal child, encouraging us to remember that nonverbal does not mean noncommunicative and that as educators we must can ensure that every child, regardless of their communication style, has the chance to succeed.

This chapter is split into three sections:

- shyness and social anxiety;
- nonverbal communication;
- Makaton™.

SHYNESS AND SOCIAL ANXIETY

Shyness in children can have significant negative consequences. Shy children often struggle with academic performance, social interactions and emotional wellbeing. They may experience anxiety, loneliness and low self-esteem. The current understanding of shyness suggests that it is a complex trait influenced by both biological and environmental factors. Schools can play a crucial role in supporting shy children and helping them overcome these challenges

(Nyborg et al., 2023). A recent study of Hong Kong kindergarteners found a strong correlation between shyness and social anxiety (Wong and Shum, 2024).

REFLECTIVE QUESTION 12.1

In what situations do you feel shy?

How can we help others overcome shyness?

Shyness and social anxiety are distinct but related concepts. Shyness involves wariness and self-consciousness in social situations, while social anxiety is characterised by excessive fear of social evaluation. Both can lead to social disengagement and emotional reactivity. Research suggests a connection between shyness and social anxiety. Heightened shyness in early childhood can predict the development of social anxiety disorder. Understanding these relationships can help educators identify and support shy and socially anxious children (Wong and Shum, 2024).

REFLECTIVE QUESTION 12.2

What are all of the other ways you can think of that we can communicate apart from speech?

STRATEGIES TO SUPPORT SHY CHILDREN

Teachers commonly use a variety of strategies to address shyness in the classroom. Studies have found that teachers frequently employ social learning techniques, such as encouragement, praise and modelling, to support shy students. They also often use peer-focused strategies, involving classmates in problem-solving or encouraging social interaction.

High-powered strategies, like punishment or direct intervention, are less common with shy students. As teachers we need to recognise the sensitive nature of shyness and thus use more therapeutic and supportive approaches. A positive and inclusive classroom environment is crucial for helping shy children feel comfortable and engaged.

Teachers primarily use three strategies to manage shy students' anxiety:

- assessing needs for seating;
- discussing feelings and behaviour;
- offering availability.

Seating arrangements seem to be the most effective. Less used strategies include early-day meetings and allowing recess breaks. These are rated as least useful, along with remaining quiet during discussions (Nyborg et al., 2023). Overall, teachers' strategies for addressing shyness are generally supportive and focus on fostering social skills and self-esteem. These approaches can help shy children feel more confident and included in the classroom environment (ibid.).

LINK TO CLASSROOM PRACTICE: ACTIVE LISTENING

Model with your class how to listen actively: explain that when someone is talking to us, some ways we can show the speaker that we are interested in what they have to say are through making eye contact, nodding and asking questions.

Pair children up and ask them to each talk for 20 seconds on something they enjoy, and the other person just has to listen actively.

You could then ask pairs to feedback to the class what their partner spoke about.

Some simple starter topics could include: explain your favourite meal, talk about a favourite toy, or describe one of your favourite places you have visited and why it was so special.

In older children and young people, we may see socially shy children finding connections in online spaces as an easier way to communicate with peers. Digital addiction is linked to loneliness, shyness and social anxiety in adolescents. A study found that these factors are positively correlated and predict social anxiety (Ime et al., 2024). Educational interventions can help address these issues.

COMMUNICATION BARRIERS

There are other reasons that a child may find it difficult to communicate apart from shyness. Lauren Tickner, Primary Education Graduate, explains 'communication barriers can occur in various environmental settings and can affect anyone, regardless of whether the person is neurodivergent or not'.

Dr Rani (2016) describes communication barriers as anything that prevents us from comprehending an intended message from another attempting to convey their ideas or thoughts or give us information. Five barriers can affect a person's ability to communicate: attitudinal, behavioural, cultural, language and environmental. Some people may come across intersectionality between these barriers, whereas some might only find one barrier when communicating. For example, a person might have a solid ability to communicate in their first language and need additional aid when translating and comprehending in their second.

In the following section, we explore further some of the influences and support systems for children who are nonverbal.

NONVERBAL COMMUNICATION

Nonverbal communication plays a crucial role in human interaction, conveying messages beyond words. The second section of this chapter explores the various aspects of nonverbal communication, from its biological and cultural influences to its specific codes and functions.

Biological and cultural influences

- *Bio-evolutionary perspective*: Nonverbal behaviour is influenced by both nature and nurture. Biological factors such as genetic traits and physiological responses contribute to our nonverbal expressions.
- *Sociocultural influences*: Cultural norms and values shape how we use and interpret nonverbal cues. Different cultures may have distinct expectations for body language, facial expressions and personal space.

Nonverbal code

- *Kinesics*: Body movements, facial expressions and eye behaviour are essential components of nonverbal communication.
- *Vocalics*: The way we speak, including tone, pitch and pace, can convey important messages.
- *Haptics*: Touch is a powerful nonverbal tool, expressing affection, aggression, or other emotions.
- *Proxemics*: The use of personal space can indicate social relationships and cultural norms.
- *Appearance and adornment*: Physical appearance and the use of objects can influence how we are perceived by others.
- *Environment and artefacts*: The physical setting and objects can shape nonverbal communication.
- *Chronemics*: The use of time can convey messages about cultural values and social status.

Functions of nonverbal communication

- *Expressing emotions*: Nonverbal cues can reveal our feelings and attitudes.
- *Regulating interactions*: Nonverbal communication helps manage the flow of conversation and maintain social relationships.

- *Presenting self*: Our appearance and behaviour can convey information about our identity and personality.
- *Reinforcing or contradicting verbal messages*: Nonverbal cues can emphasise or contradict what we say.

Understanding nonverbal communication

- *Cultural awareness*: Recognising cultural differences in nonverbal communication is essential for effective intercultural interaction.
- *Observational skills*: Developing the ability to notice and interpret nonverbal cues can enhance communication skills.
- *Contextual understanding*: Considering the situation and relationship between communicators can help interpret nonverbal messages accurately.

By understanding the various aspects of nonverbal communication, we can become more effective communicators and improve our interactions with others (Burgoon et al., 2021).

REFLECTIVE QUESTION 12.3

Do you know anyone who is nonverbal?

How do they prefer to communicate their needs?

How might we be able to support nonverbal learners in the classroom?

CHALLENGES IN DEFINING AND RESEARCHING NONVERBAL AND MINIMALLY VERBAL AUTISM

Defining *nonverbal* and *minimally verbal* (NV and MV) in ASD is crucial for effective research and intervention. However, inconsistent definitions and criteria have hindered progress in this area. Researchers often disagree on the specific criteria for classifying individuals as NV or MV. This can include factors like the presence of words, phonetic consistency, spoken versus gestural communication, and receptive language level. These inconsistencies make it difficult to compare outcomes across studies and develop targeted interventions.

While many toddlers under 18 months are NV or MV, it's important to distinguish between early and later childhood verbal abilities. Early intervention studies often focus on toddlers with or at risk for ASD, but more research is needed on NV and MV children in later childhood (Koegel et al., 2020).

In this valuable contribution, Mel Green offers insight into parenting her autistic, nonspeaking son.

CONTRIBUTION: THE NONVERBAL CHILD

BY MEL GREEN – LECTURER IN EDUCATION STUDIES AT THE OPEN UNIVERSITY

Sending my autistic, non-speaking son off to school each day requires strength, conviction and complete trust in the staff at his school. For six and a half hours, I don't fully know what my child is experiencing. He cannot tell me. When teaching a boy like mine, it's important for teachers to understand the immense trust that parents of nonverbal children place in you. My son's experience has taught me valuable lessons about communication and inclusion in the classroom, which I want to share.

UNDERSTANDING NONVERBAL COMMUNICATION

Nonverbal children, like my son, often communicate in ways that might not be immediately obvious. My son often uses vocalisations, and it is the pitch or tone he uses that indicates his emotions. For example, he makes the same 'eeeeee' sound, but a high-pitched 'eeee' sound can mean excitement, whereas a low-pitched 'eeee' sound can indicate sadness. While a nonverbal child may not use words, they often express themselves through gestures, facial expressions, behaviours, or the use of assistive technology. At home we have Widgit™ symbols on different household items like the doors and the fridge as well as 'core boards' with core words like 'hungry', 'toilet' or 'cuddle' to enable my son to point to these rather than speak. My son is very able to take me where he wants to go and move my arm to the thing he wants, such as sweets, the door handle or a toy he is unable to reach. I believe it is crucial that educators recognise these forms of communication and offer opportunities to develop competency in them, whichever communication tool they feel most comfortable with. All children deserve to have ways of expressing themselves.

Nonverbal does not mean noncommunicative. For example, my son uses a combination of vocalisations, visual aids and body language to convey his needs and feelings, and this means both us, as his parents, and his teachers, need to be observant and responsive.

Autism isn't a learning difficulty; it is a neurological condition, and it is challenging to have those that don't understand autism and nonverbal communication ask me in front of my son 'why doesn't he talk?' or 'what's wrong with him?' My son is able to follow instructions, sit for the reading of a story and engage in singing. This highlights the importance of not underestimating a child's intelligence or abilities just because they are non-speaking. My son, like many other nonverbal children, understands far more than he can express.

EFFECTIVE PARTNERSHIPS WITH PARENTS

One of my biggest concerns as a parent of a non-speaking child is having to place a lot of trust in those who are responsible for his care at school. For instance, when my son came home from school with a bite mark on his shoulder, he couldn't tell me what had happened; by the time I noticed, it was too late to follow up immediately with the staff. That night, my husband and I were incredibly fearful and running through worst-case scenarios about what had happened. As non-speaking children are unable to fill parents in about their school day, educators need to develop an effective home–school partnership and communication structure so that parents can feel safe in the knowledge that they develop strong, trusting relationships with parents and carers. Regular detailed updates and clear communication can help bridge the gap that nonverbal children cannot fill themselves.

CREATING A SUPPORTIVE ENVIRONMENT

Beyond communication strategies, fostering an inclusive environment where nonverbal children feel valued is key. In the classroom, using tools like Picture Exchange Communication System (PECS™), Widgit, Makaton, British Sign Language (BSL) or another sign language, or alternative augmented communication (AAC) technology tools can make a significant difference. Essentially, it is the educators' role to ensure the children in their class have a means by which they can communicate to them and their peers.

Additionally, and this is something I feel very strongly about, educators should always recognise and nurture each child's unique abilities by taking a strengths-based approach acknowledging a child's strengths and positives, not just focusing on what they cannot do – as this helps create a more inclusive and supportive learning environment. This means understanding that

(Continued)

every child experiences the world differently. Educators should embrace these differences, not just as challenges to be overcome, but as strengths that enrich the classroom community. My hope is that teachers see the potential in nonverbal children like my son and support them in a way that allows them to thrive.

Teaching a nonverbal child like my son comes with unique challenges, but it also offers incredible opportunities for growth and learning. By understanding nonverbal communication, building trust with parents and creating an inclusive environment, educators can ensure that every child, regardless of their communication style, has the chance to succeed. As a parent, my greatest hope is that my son's teachers see his potential and help him shine.

LINK TO CLASSROOM PRACTICE: SOCIAL STORIES

Have you used *social stories* with your class?

Social stories are narrative tools used in education to teach social skills and expectations to children, especially those with ASD or other social communication difficulties. They are designed to help these children understand social situations, rules and behaviours in a way that is clear, predictable and supportive.

How social stories are used in schools:

- *teaching social skills*: social stories can be used to teach specific social skills, such as how to greet someone, share toys, or handle conflict;
- *preparing for social situations*: they can help children prepare for new or challenging social situations, such as starting a new school or attending a party;
- *building empathy*: social stories can help children understand the feelings and perspectives of others, promoting empathy and understanding;
- *reducing anxiety*: by providing a clear and predictable framework, social stories can help reduce anxiety and improve social interactions for children with ASD.

MAKATON

In the third and final section of this chapter, we consider the tool Makaton for communicating with our learners. A helpful contribution comes from Lauren Tickner.

CONTRIBUTION: COMMUNICATION BARRIERS AND RESPONSES

BY LAUREN TICKNER – PRIMARY EDUCATION GRADUATE, QTS

WHAT IS MAKATON?

Makaton is among the most popular communication methods in the UK. This unique language programme uses a combination of signs, symbols and speech to aid communication (The Makaton Charity, 2022). Created by speech therapist Margaret Walker, it has grown in popularity since its initial rollout in the 1970s (Vinales, 2013). Since the 1970s, Makaton and the environment in which it is used have changed drastically. Initially intended to be used in psychological institutions, Walker designed the Makaton vocabulary to make communication between nurses and patients more manageable. Since then, Makaton has been developed and adapted frequently (Walker, 1987) to suit various environments (The Makaton Charity, 2022). Although the pedagogical approach has deviated from its original design, it has become a popular theory for use in educational settings, particularly those with SEND (Sheehy and Duffy, 2009).

The concept behind Makaton stems from BSL. BSL is another AAC language programme primarily used by the deaf community to facilitate peer communication (British Sign, 2023). In contrast to Makaton, BSL relies solely on visual, gestural language paired with handshapes, facial expressions and body language to help convey meaning (British Deaf Association, 2022). BSL relies heavily on bodily movements such as gestures and facial expressions. However, it is not always appropriate or inclusive for those with SEND, who may find it challenging to emulate large gestures and body language (Dyspraxia Foundation, 2023; Cerebral Palsy, 2023).

USING MAKATON TO BREAK DOWN THE BARRIERS

Since the 1970s, Makaton has been used in various environments. This can be attributed to the changing societal legislation and attitudes, such as the Equality Act (Government Legislation, 2010). This Act aimed to 'eliminate discrimination', while the Human Rights Act (The National Archives, 1998)

(Continued)

emphasised communication as a fundamental human right. AAC methods, such as Makaton, have been further thrust into broader society through supplementary resources and guidance published on government websites (gov.uk, 2015). This has allowed for the integration of inclusive behaviours in society as business owners, charities and trusts can refer to guidance when necessary.

When Makaton is available and used in everyday activities, it provides opportunities for those with communication barriers to communicate with their peers and be included in the broader society. Having the capability to communicate effectively plays a huge role in everyday life (Daly-Cano et al., 2015), as effective communication helps convey the needs and wants for the desired outcome (Stodden et al., 2003). SEND children often find communicating in a new environment with unfamiliar people anxiety-inducing (Bierman and Erath, 2007), limiting their ability to advocate for their needs. Therefore, making an AAC system like Makaton readily available to everyone can help reduce or even eliminate communication barriers.

Although Makaton has been known to positively impact individuals, its use within a whole classroom has not always been seamless. The 1987 study by Walker (1987) investigated mainstream teachers' attitudes around Makaton, with the majority indicating an unfavourable opinion (Sheehy and Duffy, 2009). Throughout this study, teacher participants often expressed how Makaton was useless when considering the context of the whole classroom setting. In the 1987 study, Walker (1987) noted that teachers' beliefs on the successful integration of SEND children were dependent on SEND children adapting to be 'more normal' (Mittler, 2000).

The use of Makaton is currently elective and not a requirement in the everyday routine of the classroom. It is up to the teacher and other supporting bodies, such as speech and language therapists, to decide if Makaton is a suitable intervention for individuals or the whole class. In mainstream schools, Makaton is often implemented for the specific benefit of one child. The language programme is exclusively used between the child and their communication partner; this could be their one-to-one teaching assistant.

To summarise, Makaton can be used to support all children, regardless of their age or ability level. Here are some ways Makaton can be used to benefit all children:

- *as a tool for communication*: Makaton can be used to express needs, thoughts and feelings, both in spoken and written language;
- *to support learning*: Makaton can be used to teach new vocabulary, concepts, and social skills;
- *to promote inclusion*: Makaton can help create a more inclusive environment where all children feel valued and supported;
- *to enhance social skills*: Makaton can help children develop social skills, such as turn-taking, sharing and cooperation;
- *to boost confidence*: Makaton can help children feel more confident in their ability to communicate and express themselves.

Overall, Makaton is a versatile communication tool that can benefit children of all ages and abilities. It can be used in various settings, including schools, Early Years settings and therapy sessions. By incorporating Makaton into educational programmes, we can create more inclusive and supportive learning environments for all children.

LINK TO CLASSROOM PRACTICE: CLASSROOM GREETINGS

How do you greet your students when they arrive for their lessons? Here are some ways teachers and teaching assistants can greet children at the classroom door to continue to foster a safe, supportive space:

- *personalise greetings*: use the child's name and ask about their day or weekend;
- *make eye contact*: show that you aree paying attention and engaged;
- *offer a warm smile*: a friendly smile can make children feel welcome and at ease;
- *give a high-five or handshake*: a physical touch can create a sense of connection;
- *use positive affirmations*: encourage children with positive statements like 'I'm so glad you're here today' or 'you're going to have a great day'.

By making a conscious effort to greet children warmly and personally as they enter our classrooms, teachers can create a positive and welcoming classroom atmosphere that helps students feel valued and supported.

SUMMARY

- Explore strategies to create supportive environments, foster social skills and build self-esteem in shy children.
- Consider nonverbal communication methods such as facial expressions, gestures, body language and the use of assistive technology.
- Explore the importance of recognising and supporting these alternative forms of communication.
- Reflect on your experiences with nonverbal individuals and consider the challenges they may face.
- Explore strategies for supporting nonverbal learners, such as using assistive technology, providing opportunities for communication and creating an inclusive classroom environment.

13

WELLBEING TIPS

INTRODUCTION

This final chapter considers ways to nurture wellbeing in all children through a range of methods, activities and spaces, and also creates space to consider how you care for your own wellbeing. It also contains thoughtful contributions encouraging further reflection on how we can ensure wellbeing is at the centre of our planning and practice to best support our learners and ourselves along our lifelong learning journeys.

DEFINING WELLBEING AND UNDERSTANDING SELF-CARE

Earlier in this book we looked at mental health and focused on how to support children with anxiety and depression (Chapter 5). This chapter looks at wellbeing, which can be seen as a very different concept to mental health.

REFLECTIVE QUESTION 13.1

How do you define the term 'wellbeing'?

'Wellbeing' can be seen as an umbrella term for the balance on which our daily function and wellness exist; when we nurture our wellbeing, our quality of life is higher, our daily functioning is better and our relationships with others and, importantly, ourselves are healthier.

The Department of Health (DoH, 2024: 1) defines wellbeing as: 'a positive state of mind and body, underpinned by social and psychological wellbeing. It enables and supports good relationships, improved resilience, improved health, meaning, purpose and control.'

To help feel more well, we need to make space and time for *self-care*, which literally means caring for ourselves in ways that makes us feel calm or happy; accordingly, then, each person's understanding of self-care may vary as we each find enjoyment in different things. Self-care can also involve simple, surface activities, such as taking a hot shower, or a warm bath, or deeper, more meaningful work such as using talking therapy to help reflect upon events or behaviours from our past to help unpack them and the influence that these have had on our lives.

REFLECTIVE QUESTION 13.2

What does self-care look like for you when you are at home?

Consider the things that bring you joy and help restore you when you are at home; are they activities and things indoors, or things to do outdoors, or a mix of both? Reflect on whether you think these things were the same ways you used for self-care when you were younger or have your self-care techniques changed over time?

Think also about the ways that you find solace when things seem difficult or challenging; does it help you to be around people, or to be alone, or does it depend on the situation? Remember that our learners will go through a range of emotions just like us. How can our spaces best meet their needs when they are feeling frustrated or overwhelmed, especially when we need to still keep them safe within the walls of our classrooms and schools?

REFLECTIVE QUESTION 13.3

What does self-care look like for you when you are at work?

Now consider how your self-care changes when you are at work. If you work in a school, the time spent by yourself – or for yourself – is likely vastly reduced. Workload may mean that you have less time for breaks, but it is important you take time to eat and drink properly, and not forget about self-care and wellbeing – even in the work space. One big change we may see between home and work is the chance to be outdoors. Let us consider further how being outdoors can positively nurture our wellbeing.

THE ROLE OF THE OUTDOORS IN OUR WELLBEING

Research shows that there are direct and indirect benefits on children and young people's wellbeing through being around and in nature (Arola et al., 2023); this can be titled *nature connectedness*. Being exposed to greenspace can support development in both physical and mental health through a range of ways: physical exercise; social cohesion; the restoration of attention; and decreasing stress (Sakhvidi et al., 2023).

Think of a typical school day in the classroom and consider how long each day is spent outdoors? Apart from the break time and lunchtime, and possibly the physical education (PE) lesson, are there other opportunities to be found to take the class outdoors?

LINK TO CLASSROOM PRACTICE: MINDFUL RAINBOW WALK

Encourage your class to truly be mindful as they acknowledge their surroundings by taking them on a *rainbow walk*. Depending on the age of your learners and the equipment available to you, you could do this in several ways.

Either:

- put children in groups and give each group a colour of the rainbow, asking them to spot and list things around the school and grounds of their colour;
- give children a picture of a rainbow and ask them to collect things in the school grounds they find or spot in that colour and write or draw onto the rainbow template.

Give each learner or pair a camera or tablet with a camera and ask them to go around the school and grounds and take a photo of one thing for each colour of the rainbow; they could then use an app to make these into a collage to print or share with the class on the whiteboard.

This rainbow walk activity helps us to be mindful – meaning present in the moment and aware of our emotions, whatever they may be.

In the first contribution in this chapter, Lou Lionetti shares an overview of the powerful benefits of mindfulness for children.

CONTRIBUTION: THE POWER OF MINDFULNESS FOR CHILDREN

BY LOU LIONETTI, VP DIGITAL TECHNOLOGIES AND ENGINEERING

Children often face the same pressures and stresses as adults in a world filled with distractions. This is where mindfulness, a simple yet powerful practice, can make a remarkable difference. Mindfulness involves paying full attention to the present moment, whether it's noticing the feeling of your breath, the sound of birds outside, or the taste of your favourite snack. When children practise mindfulness, they learn to focus, manage their emotions and find calm in the midst of chaos.

COGNITIVE BENEFITS

Research has shown that mindfulness can significantly improve a child's ability to concentrate. A study by the University of California, Los Angeles (UCLA), found that children who participated in mindfulness programmes showed better attention and focus in the classroom than those who did not. This is particularly important as attention is a key component of learning. By enhancing their ability to focus, children can absorb and retain information more effectively, leading to improved academic performance.

EMOTIONAL REGULATION

Mindfulness also plays a crucial role in emotional regulation. A study published in the journal *Mindfulness* (Phan et al., 2022) highlighted that children who engaged in regular mindfulness practices exhibited lower levels of anxiety and depression. These children were also better equipped to handle negative emotions, showing greater resilience in the face of stress. This is because mindfulness teaches children to observe their thoughts and feelings without judgement, allowing them to respond to emotions more thoughtfully rather than reacting impulsively.

SOCIAL AND EMOTIONAL LEARNING (SEL)

Incorporating mindfulness into children's routines can also enhance their social and emotional learning (SEL). According to a Collaborative for Academic, Social, and Emotional Learning (CASEL) report (2024), mindfulness practices can foster empathy and compassion in children. When children practise mindfulness, they become more aware of their own emotions and the emotions of others, which can lead to better relationships with peers and a more positive school environment.

PHYSICAL AND PSYCHOLOGICAL WELLBEING

Beyond cognitive and emotional benefits, mindfulness also supports children's physical and psychological wellbeing. Regular mindfulness practice has been linked to lower stress hormone cortisol levels, which can reduce stress-related physical symptoms like headaches and stomach-aches. Additionally, mindfulness has been found to improve sleep quality in children, which is essential for their overall health and development.

PRACTICAL APPLICATIONS

Mindfulness can be practised in various forms, such as deep breathing exercises, guided imagery, or even mindful walking. These practices can be easily integrated into daily routines. For example, a simple breathing exercise where children focus on the sensation of their breath entering and leaving their bodies can help them calm down during stressful moments. Guided imagery, where children visualise a peaceful place, can be used before bedtime to promote relaxation and better sleep.

The benefits of mindfulness for children are profound and far-reaching. Not only does it help them navigate the challenges of growing up, but it also equips them with lifelong skills that contribute to their overall wellbeing. By incorporating mindfulness into their daily lives, children can develop the ability to stay present, manage their emotions and connect with themselves and others meaningfully. This is mindfulness's gift – a foundation for a happier, healthier life.

LINK TO CLASSROOM PRACTICE: MINDFUL LEMONS!

This activity can be done with lemons or other objects that appear the same as a collective but are in fact all very different up close, such as conkers, or pebbles that you could collect for free. Show the class the bowl or bag filled with the lemons (or whichever object you choose).

Ask what it is: a bag of lemons.

(Continued)

Now give each child a lemon and ask them to truly study it for two minutes. Look at every bump, discolouration or freckle on their lemon.

Then, ask the class to either put all the lemons in the middle of their group, or – if you're feeling confident – ask all class members to come and put their lemon on a desk at the front.

Mix them up, and then ask everyone to come and find their original lemon.

You may be surprised that, hopefully, they should all identify their lemon!

A way to check is if you also have a lemon for yourself and if all students pick correctly, then just your lemon should be left.

What does this teach us? To look carefully to the smaller details in life; to slow down and be mindful and notice things around us.

Another activity known to support our wellbeing is the practice of yoga; over recent years we have seen many classrooms incorporate short yoga sessions into the weekly timetables. In this next contribution, Claire O'Neill offers a piece outlining the advantages of yoga and mindfulness in education.

CONTRIBUTION: CONNECTING THE BODY, MIND AND SOUL IN EDUCATION

BY CLAIRE O'NEILL – TEACHER AND RESEARCHER AT THE COLLEGE OF ARTS, CELTIC STUDIES AND SOCIAL SCIENCES, UNIVERSITY COLLEGE CORK

In my 25 years of teaching, practices like yoga and mindfulness have been integral not only to my self-care, but also to my teaching practice. Over time, I have built on these practices through further training and research. In this brief overview, we will explore the advantages of yoga and mindfulness in education, some common pitfalls, key considerations for teachers wishing to use these practices and, finally, some tips for success.

Certainly, there is an increasing interest in practices like yoga and mindfulness in education and this is in large part due to the positive results achieved by engaging meaningfully with these practices (Hart et al., 2022; Phan et al., 2022).

This interest exemplifies a shift away from the preferencing of top-down strategies as seen in Figure 13.1 below. Nonetheless, misconceptions and misunderstanding regarding yoga and mindfulness are rife (Leggett, 2022; Narasimhachari and Jayalakshmi, 2020). These complex practices cannot be reduced to a simple explanation. They certainly are not merely an exercise programme or a fun filler, nor are they a panacea for all support needs.

WHY USE YOGA AND MINDFULNESS?

It is perhaps overly simplistic to group strategies into neat categories like bottom-up and top-down as seen in Figure 13.1 (created by author). However, these are useful distinctions when examining the value of practices like yoga and mindfulness in education. In general terms, bottom-up strategies use the body and breath to support the learner in some way, most frequently in co- or self-regulating. In contrast, top-down strategies rely on higher-order processes like language, logic and reasoning for regulation and problem-solving.

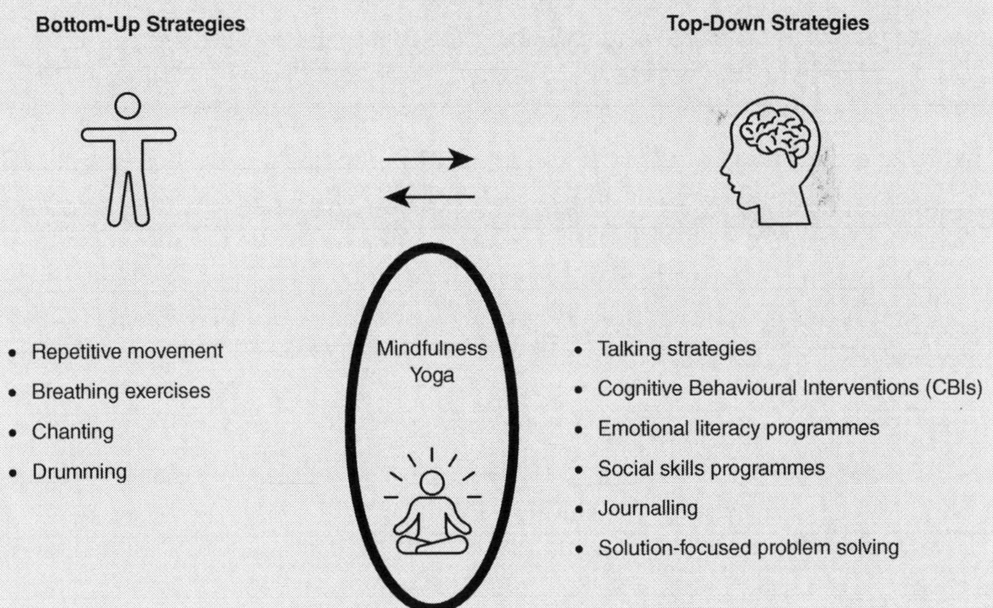

Figure 13.1 *Some* examples of bottom-up and top-down strategies

(Continued)

As holistic practices, both yoga and mindfulness usually have a blend of bottom-up and top-down elements and this combination helps connect the body and mind. Indeed, the term 'yoga' derives from a Sanskrit term meaning communion. The holistic body–mind aspect of yoga and mindfulness aligns very well with theoretical frames currently influencing pedagogic practice including the *learning pyramid* (Taylor and Trott, 1996), *polyvagal theory* (Porges, 2009) and the *neuro-sequential model* (Perry, 2019).

PITFALLS

Pitfalls can arise when these practices are poorly understood and/or poorly applied in educational settings. The following points will help teachers to avoid some common difficulties:

- teachers need to understand and teach these practices from a baseline of personal practice. Personal practice needs to be supplemented by suitable training and planning in line with school policies and curriculum;
- these practices need to be linked to suitable goals and targets;
- be cognisant that mindfulness and yoga are not suitable for every learner at every time and need to be adapted and individualised;
- avoid the potential of causing more harm than good with these practices that are intended to support. This type of harm is known as *iatrogenic harm* (Foulkes and Stringaris, 2023). Examples include using yoga asanas with learners that are hypermobile and body work with learners that have different sensory experiences without prior consideration and adaptation.

REFLECTION

The following questions highlight some important pedagogical considerations for teachers wishing to explore practices like yoga and mindfulness with their learners.

- What is your level of readiness as a practitioner?
- Are these suitable practices to engage in with your learners and in your educational context?

- What adaptations need to be made for individual learners?
- Do you have adequate resources, time and space?
- Is there outside expertise available? If so, what considerations, for example, safeguarding, need to be looked at?

TIPS

Finally, here are some tips for teachers who are already using these practices with learners or for teachers who are ready to start.

- Start small and simple. Baby steps lead to success!
- Create a safe space and time to practice. This includes a *do not disturb* sign on the door and clear instructions in advance of practice.
- Be learner-centred at all times.
- Explore adapted forms of yoga and mindfulness and/or practices with shared features. Examples include mindful colouring, Zentangle™, drumming and chanting circles, mindful movement, progressive muscular relation, noticing and savouring activities, breathing exercises and guided meditation.
- Create home school links; this will help embed the practice.

LINK TO CLASSROOM PRACTICE: WEEKLY MINDFUL MOMENTS

Having read the previous section with tips for yoga, mindfulness or movement, think about your weekly timetable.

What can you factor in to each day to give opportunities for noticing, breathing, or relaxing?

Can you timetable in one activity per day, such as a breathing activity to start your maths lesson? Or yoga before home time?

Can you print out mindful colouring pages and have them ready for a wet play?

In this next contribution, Kelsie Lee shares practical advice for teachers on simple adaptations in our classrooms and in our behaviours to help nurturing wellbeing for our learners and for ourselves.

CONTRIBUTION: NURTURING WELLBEING

BY KELSIE LEE – TRAINER TEACHER

Children's experiences in school are understood to be significant influencers for their wellbeing because they spend such a large proportion of their childhood in school (DfE, 2024). These school experiences are heavily influenced by teacher wellbeing, since children spend the majority of their time in school with their teachers. As a result, teacher wellbeing influences children's wellbeing and, subsequently, their academic achievement through the theory of social contagion (Madigan and Kim, 2021; Mercer and Gregersen, 2020).

Therefore, it is vital that we, as educators, mirror the highest levels of wellbeing that we want the children in our care to experience. We can do this by making slight adaptations to our everyday routines with the children. Listed below are some examples that you could try out in your classroom to demonstrate your own good wellbeing, to help instil this in the children in your class.

Greet every child in the playground/at the classroom door in the morning with a big smile and ask how they are doing. It is understandable that this might be quite time-consuming, so if you are lucky enough to have more than one adult in your class, share this responsibility between all of you. This simple action helps to identify any children who may already not be feeling quite themselves, allowing you to be able to support them from the very beginning of the day. Addressing negative feelings from the outset will increase the likelihood of being able to help support this child and improve their mood for the rest of the day, which saves you time in the long run.

Build strong, meaningful relationships with every child from the outset. You would not have chosen to be a teacher if you did not want to build genuine bonds with the children in your classroom. Ignite this passion! The motivation of children and teachers is tightly intertwined in a reciprocal relationship, whereby teacher motivation is not only a benefit for self-wellbeing, but also for children's wellbeing (Field, 2019; Split et al., 2011). Hence your relationships with the children strongly determine the emotional climate in your classroom.

Display positive affirmations around your classroom. Refer to these constantly throughout the school day and build them into your general practice. This way the children will see and understand how much you value them yourself as the teacher, and they will do so too.

Create an emotions board. It might be worth taking some time to think about where you display this in the classroom. No child is going to be honest with expressing a negative feeling if the display is at the very front of the classroom for everyone to see. This could be the very first thing the children do when they arrive in school. By putting this in a safe space in the classroom, it will allow any children who might not honestly answer how they are feeling when you ask them at the door, to note their feelings on a board that they know their teacher will pay attention to. It offers children a more private way of communicating with the adults in their classroom.

It is important to note that good wellbeing is recognised to be more than just the absence of ill-being (WHO, 2022). Wellbeing is fostered through a balance of positive and negative emotional experiences (Steptoe, 2019). It is about learning how to deal with these experiences, so we can look after ourselves in all contexts of life.

Listed below are some ways in which you can foster a classroom culture that celebrates mistake-making throughout the learning process.

- As the teacher, include mistakes in your demonstrations. Not only does this check if the children are paying attention to what you are teaching them and checks their understanding of the learning, it also shows that mistakes are valued and anyone can make them.
- Break tasks down into more manageable steps and reward the achievement of these. This helps to build children's resilience if they can see that they are making progress throughout the learning journey and not just being celebrated at the very end when they have completed the entire task correctly.
- Create a culture in which children enjoy helping each other to fix their mistakes. Perhaps use a buddy system. Learning to provide emotional support to each other, as well as ourselves, is key in promoting good wellbeing.

There is also a link between wellbeing and learning to cope. In this next contribution, Liz Bowles and Jayne Carter share insight into resilience and coping skill development.

CONTRIBUTION: WELLBEING FOR CHILDREN – COPING SKILLS

BY LIZ BOWLES AND JAYNE CARTER – PROJECT MANAGERS

> Modern life can be full of challenges for our children. We can't change this, but we can help children to develop the skills they will need to cope with life's difficulties, to understand and manage their emotions and to develop resilience.
>
> (Partnership for Children, n.d.)

As children spend so much of their time in your classroom, you can play a key role in helping them develop resilience and coping skills. Resilience is described as 'our ability to cope with difficult situations' (Rice, 2022), with studies showing that the development of a resilient mindset affects life by responding positively to either potential barriers or developed barriers. All children will have to deal with problems, changes and losses in their lives, so it is vital that we help them to develop the skills to cope with difficult situations. The importance of nurturing coping strategies has been proved to enable children to regulate their own feelings, choose independent tools and increase the likelihood of emotional equilibrium. Although it often feels like the right thing to do is to try to fix problems for children, it is better to encourage them to think independently and choose their own coping strategies as each of their needs and situations will be different. We should also encourage them to try out a variety of coping strategies for different situations rather than relying on a single strategy which may not always be appropriate. By using this method, children can start to build up a bank of coping strategies for themselves, as well as the confidence of knowing which can be used at particular times.

Talking openly and sensitively about difficult situations they may be experiencing can help children to process their thoughts and be less worried about them. Initially, even understanding that they are experiencing a range of feelings can help them find ways to cope. This acknowledgement provides the starting point of the coping process. You can use questions to guide children to evaluate and reflect on the effectiveness of their coping strategies. Explicitly using the language of feelings and emotions, as well as repetition and summarising of situations, are also valuable and effective strategies to use. If a child suffers a bereavement, we would also encourage you to share difficult situations you have faced. This will help children to understand that difficult situations are part of life, but we can develop the resilience and coping skills to be able to navigate them successfully.

In our programmes, children evaluate their coping strategies using two simple rules: the coping strategy must make them feel better and must not harm the child themselves or anyone else. Providing a model and structure for children to evaluate their own coping strategies helps children continuously reflect, make choices and find the most effective solution for them.

There will be many opportunities for you to encourage children to practice coping strategies within the curriculum and the pattern of a school day. For example, during transition times (such as between classes, year groups or schools) visual timetables and personalised picture planners have shown to be helpful in sequencing events and information. These reduce the cognitive load the child is accessing and can help with overwhelming feelings, helping a child to feel more balanced. A balanced feeling then enables children to make clearer choices. Planned activities also have an important role in the development of coping skills, especially effective when they include aspects of critical thinking, problem solving and collaborative discussion. In our programmes, we provide a wealth of activities, whole-class and small-group, which guide children to explore scenarios, set out possible solutions and agree on a shared conclusion. For example, the solution card sort activity provides a way for children to discuss with their friends which solutions would be helpful and which would be less helpful. Explaining their reasons helps their individual coping toolkit to grow, ready to be used if needed.

Partnership for Children's vision (n.d.) is a world in which the development of mental health and emotional resilience is part of life for every child – at home, at school and in the community. Over the last 23 years, over 2 million children around the world have taken part in the Partnership's Skills for Life programmes.

More information can be found on our website: www.partnershipforchildren.org.uk/

PLANNING FOR LIFELONG WELLBEING

The importance of helping children learn to understand wellbeing and self-care is clear when we consider how children will go on to face many changes and adversities in further life; part of our role as an educator can be helping them develop skills and strategies for resilience and coping with change. In this thoughtful contribution, Saranne Haley shares findings from supporting Year 7 pupils with the transition from primary school to secondary school through equipping them with mindfulness skills.

CONTRIBUTION: MINDFULNESS AS A COPING TOOL FOR SCHOOL ADJUSTMENT

BY SARANNE HALEY, PHD IN EDUCATION – POSTGRADUATE RESEARCHER AT THE UNIVERSITY OF BIRMINGHAM

The transition from primary to secondary school, a period in the life of every school pupil in the UK, has been established by extensive research as a potential source of stress (e.g. Evans et al., 2018). However, the case study research I conducted with Year 7 pupils as they moved up to secondary school suggested it was not the transition that they found stressful, but the adjustment to the increased expectations of secondary school life. Their wellbeing was measured using the Office for National Statistics wellbeing questions (Dolan and Metcalfe, 2012); their coping self-efficacy (the confidence they had in their ability to cope) was measured using the coping self-efficacy scale (Chesney et al., 2006). This questionnaire data was gathered after half a term, in the middle of the school year, and at the start of the last half-term of Year 7 for two cohorts, measured one year apart. For both cohorts the wellbeing and coping self-efficacy levels were high after their transition into Year 7, after half a term. These levels then fell, at the third measurement for Cohort 1 and at the second measurement for Cohort 2. This finding is supported by previous research by Symonds and Galton (2014), who found that wellbeing can fall at any point in the first year of secondary school. This suggests that school adjustment should be further prioritised through research, to better understand how we can support pupils through this sensitive period.

One way in which schools can support their pupils through school adjustment is the teaching of mindfulness. In this case study, pupils were taught mindfulness for a term in Year 7, using the .b programme (MiSP, 2009). Some pupils from each cohort were interviewed about their coping methods and the majority discussed using the mindfulness skills they had learnt for a range of difficulties, including to cope with the increased pressures associated with school adjustment. Pupils discussed using mindfulness to help them with: homework, 'if I'm stressed, like with homework and stuff' ('Ivan'); tests, 'I think definitely if I've got like a test coming up' ('India'); and exams. 'Walter' felt that using mindfulness as a class before an exam was helpful, as he recalled: 'so we all did that before the science test and yeah, it was good!' 'Henry' said he always used mindfulness ahead of an exam to help with nerves, 'every time before an exam, I always do it'. Pupils felt this coping method was effective in approaching the difficulties they experienced when navigating secondary school life.

The quantitative data gathered showed an increase in wellbeing and coping self-efficacy following the decrease seen after the first half-term at secondary school. The levels for both cohorts increased to show an insignificant difference to the initial measurement, indicating that, after the impact of the stress of school adjustment, coping skills were then used effectively by pupils to regain the high levels that were first seen after their transition. While there were other coping methods used by pupils, their mindfulness skills were evidently a useful tool in their coping toolkit, with potential to help them through the sensitive first year in secondary school. By teaching effective coping skills such as mindfulness, schools can increase the likelihood of pupils reaching the end of the first year of secondary school with high levels of wellbeing, and confidence in their ability to cope with whatever challenges may lay ahead.

This chapter has hopefully made space for you to reflect on wellbeing for yourself, wellbeing tips for your classroom and wellbeing for the learners that you are teaching. Ultimately, you need to take care of yourself so that you are happy and healthy to help provide for, and support, others. Your wellbeing must be your number-one priority; and that isn't selfish, it is *essential*.

This final chapter ends, not with a chapter summary of bullet points as in the other chapters, but with poignant final prose from Dr Frazer McGlinchey PhD (Cantab.), written to end this book.

CONTRIBUTION: WHO AM I TEACHING?

BY DR FRAZER MCGLINCHEY PHD (CANTAB.)

You are teaching and supporting a wide range of individuals as part of a greater whole.

Individuals facing universal challenges which will impact all of us in unique ways.

Young people who may be carrying problems at home and beyond, which can impact how they show up for themselves, and everyone else they interact with.

They face new challenges for their attention, and their sense of self, as well as new opportunities.

Some will be able to settle and concentrate on tasks instantly; some will be preoccupied or overwhelmed in the moment.

All can develop a toolkit of ways to settle and focus, in the classroom and beyond.

None of it defines any of them.

It's not your job to 'fix' them.

They don't need to be fixed, because they're not broken.

They get stuck sometimes, like each and every one of us.

They have hard moments and difficult emotions, none of which are a reflection on their character.

Who you are is more important than what you do; coincidentally what you do is incredibly, life-affirmingly important as well.

Holding space for young people can give them a firm foundation which may be lacking elsewhere in their lives.

Show them that they belong, and are important all the time – win, learn or draw.

Simple, accessible mindfulness practices can help them and you in profound, transformative ways.

Help them to be less reactive, and more responsive.

See them as just as important as everyone else, because they are.

All the time.

Mindfulness is a powerful tool which enables all of us to be present, without judgement.

To see how resilient we all are.

Every single breath is a chance to start again for everyone in the classroom, and everywhere else.

To let go of what doesn't serve or belong to us; the stories and habits which can make us feel lesser, or helpless.

The students you are teaching are all good and kind at the heart of them, just as you are.

Just like you, they'll forget that which means they can remember.

Mindfulness is invaluable for showing them that they are all connected.

That kindness to themselves is an act of kindness to everyone else, and that kindness to others is literally good for them.

Cruelty serves none of us, and the kinder we all are the easier this gets.

It's challenging enough being a human of any age sometimes.

You are guiding, empowering and nurturing them in ways they will carry with them for the rest of their lives.

Teaching them, just as they will teach you.

Helping them to be more mindful and kinder will have the same effect on you.

Being mindful of now can help them, just as it can you, breath by breath.

REFERENCES

ADR UK (2024) *How Administrative Data can Uncover the Relationship Between Children's Health and Education.* www.adruk.org/news-publications/news-blogs/how-administrative-data-can-uncover-the-relationship-between-childrens-health-and-education/

Alexander, P. (2007) Rethinking the 'toxicity' debate: the vitality of contemporary childhood. *Education Review,* 20(1), pp. 57–64

Ali, E., Letourneau, N. and Benzies, K. (2021) Parent–child attachment: a principle-based concept analysis. *Sage Open Nursing,* 7. https://doi.org/10.1177/23779608211009000

American Psychological Association (APA) (2013) *Diagnostic and Statistical Manual of Mental Disorders.* 5th edn. Washington, DC: APA.

Andriopoulou, P. (2022) Healing attachment trauma in adult psychotherapy: the role of limited reparenting. *European Journal of Psychotherapy and Counselling,* 23(4), pp. 1–15. https://doi.org/10.1080/13642537.2021.2000465

Arola, T., Aulake, M., Ott, A., Lindholm, M., Kouvonen, P., Virtanen, P. and Paloniemi, R. (2023) The impacts of nature connectedness on children's well-being: systematic literature review. *Journal of Environmental Psychology,* 85, p. 101913. www.sciencedirect.com/science/article/pii/S027249442200158X

Azpitarte, F. and Holt, L. (2023) Failing children with special educational needs and disabilities in England: new evidence of poor outcomes and a postcode lottery at the local authority level at Key Stage 1. *British Educational Research Journal,* 50, pp. 414–37. https://bera-journals.onlinelibrary.wiley.com/doi/full/10.1002/berj.3930

Ball, S. J. (2021) *The Education Debate.* 4th edn. Bristol: Policy Press.

Bancroft, H. and Mitchell, A. (2023) Number of children living in extreme poverty nearly triples in five years. *Indepenendent,* 24 October. www.independent.co.uk/news/uk/home-news/poverty-children-dwp-energy-bills-food-b2434506.html

Benoit, D. (2004) Infant–parent attachment: definition, types, antecedents, measurement and outcome. *Paediatrics and Child Health,* 9(8), pp. 541–5. https://doi.org/10.1093/pch/9.8.541

Bergin, C. and Bergin, D. (2009) Attachment in the classroom. *Educational Psychology Review,* 21(2), 141–70. https://doi.org/10.1007/s10648-009-9104-0

Bierman, K. L. and Erath, S. A. (2007) Social anxiety and peer relations in early adolescence: behavioural and cognitive factors. *Journal of Abnormal Child Psychology*, 35(3), pp. 405–16. doi: 10.1007/s10802-007-9099-2

Blanco, D., Roberts, R. M., Gannoni, A. and Cook, S. (2023) Assessment and treatment of mental health conditions in children and adolescents: a systematic scoping review of how virtual reality environments have been used. *Clinical Child Psychology and Psychiatry*, 29(3), pp. 1070–82. https://journals.sagepub.com/doi/full/10.1w177/13591045231204082

Boberiene, L. V. (2013) Can policy facilitate human capital development? The critical role of student and family engagement in schools. *American Journal of Orthopsychiatry*, 83(2–3), pp. 346–51.

Boldt, L. J., Goffin, K. C. and Kochanska, G. (2020) The significance of early parent–child attachment for emerging regulation: a longitudinal investigation of processes and mechanisms from toddler age to preadolescence. *Developmental Psychology*, 56(3), p. 431. https://psycnet.apa.org/record/2020-11553-005

Bouchard, S. (2011) Could virtual reality be effective in treating children with phobias? *Expert Review of Neurotherapeutics*, 11(2), pp. 207–13. www.tandfonline.com/doi/abs/10.1586/ern.10.196

Boullier, M. and Blair, M. (2018) Adverse childhood experiences. *Paediatrics and Child Health*, 28(3), pp. 132–7.

Bowlby, J. (1982) Attachment and loss: retrospect and prospect. *American Journal of Orthopsychiatry*, 52(4), pp. 664–78. https://doi.org/10.1111/j.1939-0025.1982.tb01456.x

Bowlby, J. (1988) Caring for children. In J. Bowlby (ed.), *A Secure Base*. New York: Routledge, pp. 1–21.

Bretherton, I. (1985) Attachment theory: retrospect and prospect. *Monographs of the Society for Research in Child Development*, 50(1/2), pp. 3–35. www.jstor.org/stable/3333824

British Deaf Association (2022) Help and resources. https://bda.org.uk/help-resources/

British Sign (2023) Home page. www.british-sign.co.uk/

Bronfenbrenner, U. (1977) Toward an experimental ecology of human development. *American Psychologist*, 32(7), p. 513.

Bronfenbrenner, U. and Evans, G. W. (2000) Developmental science in the 21st century: emerging questions, theoretical models, research designs and empirical findings. *Social Development*, 9(1), pp. 115–25.

Brophy, S., Todd, C., Rahman, M. A., Kennedy, N. and Rice, F. (2021) Timing of parental depression on risk of child depression and poor educational outcomes: a population-based routine data cohort study from Born in Wales, UK. PLOS ONE, 16(11), e0258966. https://doi.org/10.1371/journal.pone.0258966

Burešová, I., Bartošová, K. and čerňák, M. (2015) Connection between parenting styles and self-harm in adolescence. *Procedia: Social and Behavioral Sciences*, 171, pp. 1106–13. https://doi.org/10.1016/j.sbspro.2015.01.270

Burgoon, J. K., Manusov, V. and Guerrero, L. K. (2021) *Nonverbal Communication*. London: Routledge.

Byrd, D. R. and Alexander, M. (2020) Investigating special education teachers' knowledge and skills: preparing general teacher preparation for professional development. *Journal of Pedagogical Research*, 4(2), pp. 72–82.

Caballero-Julia, D., Martín-Lucas, J. and Andrade-Silva, L. E. (2024) Unpacking the relationship between screen use and educational outcomes in childhood: a systematic literature review. *Computers and Education*, 215, p. 105049.

Carlisle, D. (2022) See me, hear me: successes and challenges of students with invisible disabilities at university in Singapore. *Asia Pacific Journal of Developmental Differences*, 9(1). doi: 10.3850/S2345734122000142

CASEL (2024) *What Does the Research Say?* https://casel.org/fundamentals-of-sel/what-does-the-research-say/

Centre for Early Childhood (2021) *Big Change Starts Small*. https://assets.ctfassets.net/qwnplnakca8g/2iLCWZESD2RLu24m443HUf/1c802df74c44ac6bc94d4338ff7ac53d/RFCEC_BCCS_Report_and_Appendices.pdf

Centre for Studies on Inclusive Education (CSIE) (1994) *The UNESCO Salamanca Statement*. www.csie.org.uk/inclusion/unesco-salamanca.shtml

Cerebral Palsy Organisation (2023) *What is Cerebral Palsy?* www.cerebralpalsy.org.uk/cerebral-palsy.html

Cerna, L., Mezzanotte, C., Rutigliano, A., Brussino, O., Santiago, P., Borgonovi, F. and Guthrie, C. (2021) *Promoting Inclusive Education for Diverse Societies: A Conceptual Framework*. www.oecd-ilibrary.org/content/paper/94ab68c6-en

Chapman, E. (2023) Preventing unmet need from leading to school exclusion: empowering schools to identify neurodiversity earlier. Doctoral dissertation. University of Leeds. https://etheses.whiterose.ac.uk/33429/

Chawla, L. (2020) Childhood nature connection and constructive hope: a review of research on connecting with nature and coping with environmental loss. *People and Nature*, 2(3), pp. 619–42.

Chesney, M. A., Neilands, T. B., Chambers, D. B., Taylor, J. M. and Folkman, S. (2006) A validity and reliability study of the coping self-efficacy scale. *British Journal of Health Psychology*, 11(3), pp. 421–37.

Children's Hospital Colorado (2024) *A Parent's Guide to Neurodiversity*. www.childrenscolorado.org/conditions-and-advice/parenting/parenting-articles/neurodiversity/

Comer, J. (1995) Lecture given at Education Service Center, Region IV. Houston, TX.

Cook, A. (2024) Conceptualisations of neurodiversity and barriers to inclusive pedagogy in schools: a perspective article. *Journal of Research in Special Educational Needs*. https://nasenjournals.onlinelibrary.wiley.com/doi/full/10.1111/1471-3802.12656

Costelloe, A., Mintz, J. and Lee, F. (2020) Bereavement support provision in primary schools: an exploratory study. *Educational Psychology in Practice*, 36(3), pp. 281–96.

Cunningham, H. (2020) *Children and Childhood in Western Society since 1500*. London: Routledge.

Currigan, S. and Shackleton, E. (2022) How to create a trauma and attachment aware classroom with Rebecca Brooks. *School Behaviour Secrets* podcast. https://beaconschoolsupport.co.uk/podcast/how-to-create-a-trauma-and-attachment-aware-classroom-with-rebecca-brooks#:~:text=In%20this%20episode%2C%20author%20and,of%20creating%20success%20for%20all

Curtis, H. (2015) *Everyday Life and the Unconscious Mind*. London: Routledge.

Daly-Cano, M., Vaccaro, A. and Newman, B. (2015) College student narratives about learning and using self-advocacy skills. *Journal of Postsecondary Education and Disability*, 28(2), pp. 213–27. https://files.eric.ed.gov/fulltext/EJ1074673.pdf

De Botton, A. (ed.) (2023) *An Emotional Menagerie: An A to Z of Poems About Feelings: Feelings from A–Z*. London: School of Life.

de Souza Fleith, D., Vilarinho-Pereira, D. and Muniz Prado, R. (2024) Voices from the families: strategies for and challenges in raising a gifted child. *Journal for the Education of the Gifted*, 47(2), pp. 162–81. https://doi.org/10.1177/01623532241235576

Department for Education (DfE) (2017) *Transforming Children and Young People's Mental Health Provision: A Green Paper*. https://assets.publishing.service.gov.uk/media/5a823518e5274a2e87dc1b56/Transforming_children_and_young_people_s_mental_health_provision.pdf

DfE (2024) *Promoting and Supporting Mental Health and Wellbeing in Schools and Colleges*. www.gov.uk/guidance/mental-health-and-wellbeing-support-in-schools-and-colleges

Department of Health (DoH) (2024) *Wellbeing and Health*. assets.publishing.service.gov.uk/media/5a7c551ae5274a2041cf34cc/DH_wellbeing_health.pdf

Dolan, P. and Metcalfe, R. (2012) Measuring subjective wellbeing: recommendations on measures for use by national governments. *Journal of Social Policy*, 41, 409–27.

Duncan, D. A. (2020) Death and dying: a systematic review into approaches used to support bereaved children. *Review of Education*, 8(2), pp. 452–79. https://doi.org/10.1002/rev3.3193

Dunn, J., Bretherton, I. and Munn, P. (1987) Conversations about feeling states between mothers and their young children. *Developmental Psychology*, 23(1), p. 132.

Dykas, M. J. and Cassidy, J. (2011) Attachment and the processing of social information across the life span: theory and evidence. *Psychological Bulletin*, 137(1), pp. 19–46. https://doi.org/10.1037/a0021367

Dyspraxia Foundation (2023) *What is Dyspraxia?* https://dyspraxiafoundation.org.uk/what_is_dyspraxia/dyspraxia-at-a-glance/

Eden, C. A., Chisom, O. N. and Adeniyi, I. S. (2024a) Cultural competence in education: strategies for fostering inclusivity and diversity awareness. *International Journal of Applied Research in Social Sciences*, 6(3), pp. 383–92.

Eden, C. A., Chisom, O. N. and Adeniyi, I. S. (2024b) Parent and community involvement in education: strengthening partnerships for social improvement. *International Journal of*

Applied Research in Social Sciences, 6(3), pp. 372–82. www.fepbl.com/index.php/ijarss/article/view/894

Eley, T. C. (2015) The intergenerational transmission of anxiety: a children-of-twins study. *American Journal of Psychiatry*, 172(7), pp. 630–7. https://doi.org/10.1176/appi.ajp.2015.14070818

European Council (2018) *Council Recommendation of 22 May 2018 on Promoting Common Values, Inclusive Education, and the European Dimension of Teaching*. https://ec.europa.eu/transparency/regdoc/rep/1/2018/EN/COM-2018-23-F1-EN-MAIN-PART-1.PDF

Evans, D., Borriello, G. A. and Field, A. P. (2018) A review of the academic and psychological impact of the transition to secondary education. *Frontiers in Psychology*, 9, p. 1482.

Eyre, D. (2002) Structured tinkering: improving provision for the gifted in ordinary schools. *Gifted and Talented International*, 22(1), pp. 31–28.

Fearon, R. M. P. and Roisman, G. I. (2017) Attachment theory: progress and future directions. *Current Opinion in Psychology*, 15, pp. 131–6. https://doi.org/10.1016/j.copsyc.2017.03.002

Felitti, V. J., Anda, R. F., Nordenberg, D., Williamson, D. F., Spitz, A. M., Edwards, V., Koss, M. P. and Marks, J. S. (1998) Adverse childhood experiences study questionnaire [database record]. *PsycTESTS*. https://doi.org/10.1037/t26957-000

Felix, J. and Webb, L. (2024) *Use of Artificial Intelligence in Education Delivery and Assessment*. London: Parliamentary Office of Science and Technology. https://doi.org/10.58248/PN712

Field, J. (2019) Teacher burnout and student outcomes: is there a link and are student-teacher relationships a predictor? Doctoral thesis. University of Southampton. https://eprints.soton.ac.uk/437502/

Foulkes, L. and Stringaris, A. (2023) Do no harm: can school mental health interventions cause iatrogenic harm? *BJPsych Bulletin*, 47(5), pp. 267–9. doi: https://doi.org/10.1192/bjb.2023.9

Geddes, C. (2022) *Children and Complex Trauma: A Roadmap for Healing and Recovery*. Altona, Manitoba: FriesenPress.

Gentle, L. (2024) An examination of the attachment script assessment (ASA), mentoring script assessment (MSA), and the relationship between secure base script knowledge and mentoring script knowledge. Doctoral dissertation. Birmingham City University.

Gilbert, L., Gus, L. and Rose, J. (2021) Why do we need emotion coaching? In L. Gilbert, L. Gus and J. Rose (eds), *Emotion Coaching with Children and Young People in Schools: Promoting Positive Behaviour, Wellbeing and Resilience*. London: Jessica Kingsley, pp. 15–42.

Glasofer, D. R. (2021) *DSM-5 Criteria for Generalised Anxiety Disorder*. www.verywellmind.com/dsm-5-criteria-for-generalized-anxiety-disorder-1393147

Global Campaign for Education (2024) *The Sustainable Development Goal 4*. https://sdgs.un.org/goals/goal4

Gordon-Gould, P. and Hornby, G. (2023) *Inclusive Education at the Crossroads: Exploring Effective Special Needs Provision in Global Contexts*. London: Routledge.

gov.uk (2015) *Accessible Communication Formats*. www.gov.uk/government/publications/inclusive-communication/accessiblecommunication-formats

Government Legislation (2010) The Equality Act. www.legislation.gov.uk/ukpga/2010/15/pdfs/ukpga_20100015_en.pdf

Grant, R. J. (2023) *Play Interventions for Neurodivergent Children and Adolescents: Promoting Growth, Empowerment, and Affirming Practices*. London: Taylor & Francis.

Guy-Evans, O. (2024) *Bronfenbrenner's Ecological Systems Theory*. simplypsychology.org

Harrington, E. M., Trevino, S. D., Lopez, S. and Giuliani, N. R. (2020) Emotion regulation in early childhood: implications of socioemotional and academic components of school readiness. *American Psychological Association*, 20(1), pp. 48–53.

Hart, N., Fawkner, S., Niven, A. and Booth, J. N. (2022) Scoping review of yoga in schools: mental health and cognitive outcomes in both neurotypical and neurodiverse youth populations. *Children*, 9(6), p. 849. doi: https://doi.org/10.3390/children9060849

Hawes, D. J., Gardner, F., Dadds, M. R., Frick, P. J., Kimonis, E. R., Burke, J. D. and Fairchild, G. (2023) Oppositional defiant disorder. *Nature Reviews Disease Primers*, 9(1), p. 31. www.nature.com/articles/s41572-023-00441-6

Heckman, J. J. (2008) Schools, skills, and synapses. *Economic Inquiry*, 46, pp. 289–324.

Hope Currin, F. (2022) Supporting shy and neurodivergent children in social play. *CHI Conference on Human Factors in Computing Systems, Extended Abstracts* (pp. 1–6). April. https://dl.acm.org/doi/abs/10.1145/3491101.3503800

Hopwood, M. (2023) Anxiety symptoms in patients with major depressive disorder: commentary on prevalence and clinical implications. *Neurological Therapy*, 12(Suppl 1), pp. 5–12. doi: 10.1007/s40120-023-00469-6. Epub 2023 Apr 28. PMID: 37115459; PMCID: PMC10141876.

House of Lords (2022) *Children and Families Act 2014: A Failure of Implementation*. https://committees.parliament.uk/publications/31839/documents/179148/default/

Howes, C. and Ritchie, S. (2002) *A Matter of Trust: Connecting Teachers and Learners in the Early Childhood Classroom*. New York: Teachers College Press.

Hutchings, J., Williams, M. E. and Leijten, P. (2023) Attachment, behavior problems, and interventions. *Frontiers in Child and Adolescent Psychiatry*, 2. www.frontiersin.org/journals/child-and-adolescent-psychiatry/articles/10.3389/frcha.2023.1156407/full

Huth-Bocks, A. C., Zakir, N., Guyon-Harris, K. and Waters, H. S. (2022) Maternal secure base scripts predict child attachment security in an at-risk sample. *Infant Behaviour and Development*, 66(May 2021), pp. 1–9.

Ime, Y., Akyıl, Y. and Caglar, A. (2024) The examination of the relationships among digital addiction, loneliness, shyness, and social anxiety in adolescents. *Anales de Psicología/Annals of Psychology*, 40(2), pp. 236–41. www.researchgate.net/publication/379902594_

The_examination_of_the_relationships_among_digital_addiction_loneliness_shyness_and_social_anxiety_in_adolescents

ITU (2023) *Population of global offline continues steady decline to 2.6 billion people in 2023.* www.itu.int/en/mediacentre/Pages/PR-2023-09-12-universal-and-meaningful-connectivity-by-2030.aspx

Jones, C. (2021) *Research Commentary: Teaching About Sex, Sexual Orientation and Gender Reassignment.* www.gov.uk/government/speeches/research-commentary-teaching-about-sex-sexual-orientation-and-gender-reassignment.

Joshi, H. and Fitzsimons, E. (2016) The Millennium Cohort Study: the making of a multi-purpose resource for social science and policy. *Longitudinal and Life Course Studies*, 7(4). https://doi.org/10.14301/llcs.v7i4.410

Keller, H. (2018) Universality claim of attachment theory: children's socioemotional development across cultures. *Proceedings of the National Academy of Sciences, PNAS*, 115(45), pp. 11414–19. https://doi.org/10.1073/pnas.1720325115

Kelty, N. E. and Wakabayashi, T. (2020) Family engagement in schools: parent, educator, and community perspectives. *Sage Open*, 10(4), p. 2158244020973024. https://journals.sagepub.com/doi/full/10.1177/2158244020973024

Kent Community Health NHS Foundation Trust (2024) Neurodivergence. www.kentcht.nhs.uk/childrens-therapies-the-pod/neurodivergence/

Koegel, L. K., Bryan, K. M., Su, P. L., Vaidya, M. and Camarata, S. (2020) Definitions of non-verbal and minimally verbal in research for autism: a systematic review of the literature. *Journal of Autism and Developmental Disorders*, 50, pp. 2957–72. https://link.springer.com/article/10.1007/s10803-020-04402-w

Langley, E., Hooley, T. and Bertuchi, D. (2014) *A Career Postcode Lottery? Local Authority Provision of Youth and Career Support Following the 2011 Education Act.* https://repository.derby.ac.uk/item/92554/a-career-postcode-lottery-local-authority-provision-of-youth-and-career-support-following-the-2011-education-act

Lasater, K., Crowe, T. C. and Pijanowski, J. (2023) Developing family-school partnerships in the midst of demographic change: an examination of educators' attitudes, values, and beliefs and the discourses they shape. *Leadership and Policy in Schools*, 22(2), pp. 347–68. www.tandfonline.com/doi/abs/10.1080/15700763.2021.1958869

Le Cunff, A. L., Dommett, E. and Giampietro, V. (2024) Neurodiversity and cognitive load in online learning: a systematic review with narrative synthesis. *Educational Research Review*, 43, p. 100604. www.sciencedirect.com/science/article/pii/S1747938X24000137?via%3Dihub

Leerkes, E. M. and Augustine, M. E. (2019) Parenting and emotions. In M. H. Bornstein (ed.), *Handbook of Parenting*. London: Routledge, pp. 620–53.

Leggett, W. (2022) Can mindfulness really change the world? The political character of meditative practices. *Critical Policy Studies*, 16(3), 261–78. doi: https://doi.org/10.1080/19460171.2021.1932541

Lindsay, G., Wedell, K. and Dockrell, J. (2020) Warnock 40 years on: the development of special educational needs since the Warnock Report and implications for the future. *Frontiers in Education*, 4, p. 164. Frontiers Media SA.

Livingstone, S. (2013) Online risk, harm and vulnerability: reflections on the evidence base for child Internet safety policy. *ZER: Journal of Communication Studies*, 18(35). pp. 13–28. ISSN 1137-1102

Loomes, R., Hull, L. and Mandy, W. P. L. (2017) What Is the Male-to-Female Ratio in Autism Spectrum Disorder? A Systematic Review and Meta-Analysis. Journal of the American Academy of Child and Adolescent Psychiatry, 56(6), 466–474. https://doi.org/10.1016/j.jaac.2017.03.013

Lowe, H. and McCarthy, A. (2020) *Making Space for Able Learners. Cognitive Challenge: Principles into Practice.* Didcot: NACE. www.nace.co.uk/page/making-space-principles-into-practice

Lytje, M. and Dyregrov, A. (2023) When young children grieve. Supporting daycare children following bereavement: a parent's perspective. *OMEGA-Journal of Death and Dying*, 86(3), pp. 980–1001. https://journals.sagepub.com/doi/10.1177/0030222821997702

Lyu, X. (2023) A literature review of how children secure attachment predicts better academic performance. *Journal of Education Humanities and Social Sciences*, 8, pp. 1708–14). www.researchgate.net/publication/368377573_A_Literature_Review_of_How_Children_Secure_Attachment_Predict_Better_Academic_Performance

Madigan, D. J. and Kim, L. E. (2021) Does teacher burnout affect students? A systematic review of its association with academic achievement and student-reported outcomes. *International Journal of Educational Research*, 105, p. 101714.

McCarthy, A. (2021) *Ability Grouping: A Role in Cognitively Challenging Learning Environments?* NACE blog. www.nace.co.uk/blogpost/1761881/363563/Ability-grouping-a-role-in-cognitively-challenging-learning-environments

Mental Health Foundation (2023) *The Anxious Child.* www.mentalhealth.org.uk/explore-mental-health/publications/anxious-child

Mercer, J. (2011) Attachment theory and its vicissitudes: toward an updated theory. *Theory and Psychology*, 21(1), 25–45. https://doi.org/10.1177/0959354309356136

Mercer, S. and Gregersen, T. (2020) *Teacher Wellbeing*. Oxford: Oxford University Press.

Milton, J. (2004) Helping primary school children manage loss and grief: ways the classroom teacher can help. *Education and Health*, 22(4), pp. 58–60.

MiSP (2009) Mindfulness in Schools Project. https://mindfulnessinschools.org/

Mittler, P. (2000) *Working Towards Inclusive Education: Social Contexts.* London: David Fulton.

Moss, E. and St-Laurent, D. (2001) Attachment at school age and academic performance. *Developmental Psychology*, 37(6), pp. 863–74. www.researchgate.net/publication/11654322_Attachment_at_school_age_and_academic_performance

Mullins, L. (2024) *Supporting Neurodivergent Children and Families: A Practitioner's Guide.* London: Taylor & Francis.

Narasimhachari, R. and Jayalakshmi, A. R. (2020) Yoga and its contribution to the world. *International Journal of Health, Physical Education and Computer Science in Sports*, 16. ISSN: 2231-3265

Negru-Subtirica, O., Pop, E. and Crocetti, E. (2017) A longitudinal integration of identity styles and educational identity processes in adolescence. *Developmental Psychology*, 53(11), pp. 2127–38.

Newlove-Delgado, T., McManus, S., Sadler, K., Thandi, S., Vizard, T., Cartwright, C. and Ford, T. on behalf of Mental Health of Children and Young People Group (2021) Child mental health in England before and during the COVID-19 lockdown. *The Lancet Psychiatry*, 8(5), p. 353.

Newton, J. and Ponting, C. (2013) Eliciting young people's views on wellbeing through contemporary science debates in Wales. *Child Indicators Research*, 6, pp. 71–95. https://doi.org/10.1007/s12187-012-9159-1

NHS (2021) *Attention Deficit Hyperactivity Disorder*. www.nhs.uk/conditions/attention-deficit-hyperactivity-disorder-adhd/symptoms/

NHS (2023a) *Anxiety in Children*. www.nhs.uk/mental-health/children-and-young-adults/advice-for-parents/anxiety-in-children/

NHS (2023b) *Depression in Children and Young People*. www.nhs.uk/mental-health/children-and-young-adults/advice-for-parents/children-depressed-signs/

NHS England Digital (2018) *Mental Health of Children and Young People in England, 2017 [PAS]*. digital.nhs.uk/data-and-information/publications/statistical/mental-health-of-children-and-young-people-in-england/2017/2017

NHS England Digital (2023) *Mental Health of Children and Young People in England, 2023 - Wave 4 Follow Up to the 2017 Survey*. https://digital.nhs.uk/data-and-information/publications/statistical/mental-health-of-children-and-young-people-in-england/2023-wave-4-follow-up

NSPCC (2021) *Gender Identity*. www.nspcc.org.uk/keeping-children-safe/sex-relationships/gender-identity/

NSPCC (2024) *Children in Care*. https://learning.nspcc.org.uk/children-and-families-at-risk/looked-after-children

Nyborg, G., Mjelve, L. H., Arnesen, A., Crozier, W. R., Bjørnebekk, G. and Coplan, R. J. (2023) Teachers' strategies for managing shy students' anxiety at school. *Nordic Psychology*, 75(1), pp. 50–74.

OECD (2024) *Infant Mortality Rates*. www.oecd.org/en/data/indicators/infant-mortality-rates.html

Ofsted (1998) *Educating the Very Able: Current International Research*. OFSTED reviews of research. London: TSO.

Ofsted (2015) *Ofsted Inspection Handbook*. https://assets.publishing.service.gov.uk/government/uploads/system/uploads/attachment_data/file/390141/School_inspection_handbook.pdf

Ollendick, T. H., King, N. J. and Muris, P. (2002) Fears and phobias in children: phenomenology, epidemiology, and aetiology. *Child and Adolescent Mental Health*, 7, pp. 98–106. https://doi.org/10.1111/1475-3588.00019

Ozturk, O. and Kızılkan, T. (2024) *How Do I Support Neurodivergent Students?* British Council. www.teachingenglish.org.uk/community/magazine/how-do-i-support-neurodivergent-students

Palmer, S. (2007) *Toxic Childhood: How the Modern World is Damaging our Children and What We Can Do About It*. London: Orion.

Parker, R. and Rose, J. (2014) The implications of attachment theory for schools. *SecEd*. www.sec-ed.co.uk/content/best-practice/the-implications-of-attachment-theory-for-schools/

Parr, C. (2019) How to use attachment theory in schools: an interview with Howard Steele. *TES*, December. www.tes.com/magazine/archived/how-use-attachment-theory-schools

Partnership for Children (n.d.) *Why Our Work Matters*. www.partnershipforchildren.org.uk/who-we-are/why-our-work-matters/

Peebles, J. L., Mendaglio, S. and McCowan, M. (2023) The experience of parenting gifted children: a thematic analysis of interviews with parents of elementary-age children. *Gifted Child Quarterly*, 67(1), pp. 18–27. https://journals.sagepub.com/doi/full/10.1177/00169862221120418

Perry, B. D. (2019) The neurosequential model. In M. H. Teicher, O. Munkbaatar, A. N. Schore, K. Gatwiri, B. D. Perry, G. Kickett and S. Chandran (eds), *The Handbook of Therapeutic Care for Children: Evidence-informed Approaches to Working with Traumatized Children and Adolescents in Foster, Kinship and Adoptive Care*. London: Jessica Kingsley, pp. 137–56. ISBN: 1784505544, 9781784505547

Phan, M. L., Renshaw, T. L., Caramanico, J., Greeson, J. M., MacKenzie, E., Atkinson-Diaz, Z. and Nuske, H. J. (2022) Mindfulness-based school interventions: a systematic review of outcome evidence quality by study design. *Mindfulness*, 13(7), pp. 1591–613. doi: https://doi.org/10.1007/s12671-022-01885-9

Piaget, J. (1977) *The Development of Thought: Equilibration of Cognitive Structures*. Trans. A. Rosin. New York: Viking.

Porges, S. W. (2009) The polyvagal theory: new insights into adaptive reactions of the autonomic nervous system. *Cleveland Clinic Journal of Medicine*, 76(Suppl 2), S86. doi: 10.3949/ccjm.76.s2.17

Porter, J. (2016) Bereavement in the primary school: a critical consideration of the nature, incidence, impact and possible responses. *The STeP Journal (Student Teacher Perspectives)*, 3(1), pp. 11–17. https://insight.cumbria.ac.uk/id/eprint/2864/

Public Health England (PHE) (2020) *Oral Health Survey of 5-Year-Old Children 2019*. www.gov.uk/government/statistics/oral-health-survey-of-5-year-old-children-2019

Quinton, A., Happé, F., Fazel, M., Skripkauskaite, S. and Soneson, E. (2024) *How Is Being Neurodivergent Associated with Negative Experiences and Mental Health in Young People?* https://osf.io/by5n2/resources

Rani, U. (2016) Communication barriers. *Journal of English Language and Literature*, 3(Spl Issue 2). https://joell.in/wp-content/uploads/2016/03/74-76COMMUNICATION-BARRIERS.pdf

Ranson, K. E. and Urichuk, L. J. (2008) The effect of parent–child attachment relationships on child biopsychosocial outcomes: a review. *Early Child Development and Care*, 178(2), pp. 129–52. https://doi.org/10.1080/03004430600685282

RCPCH (2023) *RCPCH Responds to Latest Childhood Obesity Figures for England, 2022/23*. www.rcpch.ac.uk/news-events/news/rcpch-responds-latest-childhood-obesity-figures-england-202223

Rice, A. (2022) What resilience is and isn't. *PsychCentral*. https://psychcentral.com/lib/what-is-resilience#definition

Riley, P. (2011) *Attachment Theory and the Teacher–Student Relationship*. London: Routledge.

Rosa, A., Pujia, A. M., Docimo, R. and Arcuri, C. (2023) Managing dental phobia in children with the use of virtual reality: a systematic review of the current literature. *Children*, 10(11), p. 1763. https://www.mdpi.com/2227-9067/10/11/1763

Rosenshine, B. (2010) *Principles of Instruction*. Brussels: International Academy of Education.

Ruble, D. N. and Martin, C. L. (1998) Gender development. In W. Damon and N. Eisenberg (eds), *Handbook of Child Psychology: Social, Emotional, and Personality Development*. 5th edn. London: John Wiley, pp. 933–1016.

Sakhvidi, M. J. Z., Mehrparvar, A. H., Sakhvidi, F. Z. and Dadvand, P. (2023) Greenspace and health, wellbeing, physical activity, and development in children and adolescents: an overview of the systematic reviews. *Current Opinion in Environmental Science and Health*, 32, p. 100445. www.sciencedirect.com/science/article/pii/S2468584423000053

Seligman, L. D., Talavera-Garza, L. and Ollendick, T. H. (2023) Specific phobia in children and adolescents. In B. A. Bracken, L. A. Theodore and M. A. Bray (eds), *Desk Reference in School Psychology*. Oxford: Oxford University Press, pp. 324–44.

Sellers, R., Warne, N., Pickles, A., Maughan, B., Thapar, A. and Collishaw, S. (2019) Cross-cohort change in adolescent outcomes for children with mental health problems. *Journal of Child Psychology and Psychiatry*, 60, pp. 813–21. https://doi.org/10.1111/jcpp.13029

Shahar, S. and Galai, C. (2023) *Childhood in the Middle Ages*. London: Routledge.

Sheehy, K. and Duffy, H. (2009) Attitudes to Makaton in the ages on integration and inclusion. *International Journal of Special Education*, 24(2). www.eymatters.co.uk/wp-content/uploads/2020/06/sheehyDuffy2009.pdf

Split, J. L., Koomen, H. M. Y. and Thijs, J. T. (2011) Teacher wellbeing: the importance of teacher–student relationships. *Educational Psychology Review*, 23(4), pp. 457–77. https://doi.org/10.1007/s10648-011-9170-y

Spruit, A., Goos, L., Weenink, N., Rodenburg, R., Niemeyer, H., Stams, G. J. and Colonnesi, C. (2020) The relation between attachment and depression in children and adolescents: a multilevel meta-analysis. *Clinical Child and Family Psychology Review*, 23, pp. 54–69. https://link.springer.com/article/10.1007/s10567-019-00299-9

Sroufe, L. A. (2005) Attachment and development: a prospective, longitudinal study from birth to adulthood. *Attachment and Human Development*, 7(4), pp. 349–67. https://doi.org/10.1080/14616730500365928

Steffenburg, H., Steffenburg, S., Gillberg, C. and Billstedt, E. (2018) Children with autism spectrum disorders and selective mutism. *Neuropsychiatric Disease and Treatment*, 14, pp. 1163–9. https://doi.org/10.2147/NDT.S154966

Steptoe, A. (2019) Happiness and health. *Annual Review of Public Health*, 40(1), pp. 339–59.

Steven, S. (1950) *Introduction: A Definition of Communication*, 22(6), p. 689. https://doi.org/10.1121/1.1906670

Stodden, R., Conway, M. and Chang, K. (2003) Findings from the study of transition, technology and postsecondary supports for youth with disabilities: implications for secondary school educators. *Journal of Special Education Technology*, 18. 10.1177/016264340301800403

Stonewall (2023) *LGBTQ+ Inclusion in Primary Schools: How Primary Schools are Celebrating Difference and Tackling Homophobia, Biphobia and Transphobia*. www.stonewall.org.uk/system/files/lgbtq_inclusion_in_primary_schools_-_may_2023_update.pdf

Strauss, C. C. and Last, C. G. (1993) Social and simple phobias in children. *Journal of Anxiety Disorders*, 7(2), pp. 141–52. www.sciencedirect.com/science/article/abs/pii/088761859390012A

Su, X. and Yan, S. (2023) NoPhobiar: designing a VR game to prevent childhood dark phobia with children and stakeholders. *Extended Abstracts of the 2023 CHI Conference on Human Factors in Computing Systems*. April. pp. 1–6. https://dl.acm.org/doi/10.1145/3544549.3585733

Substance Abuse and Mental Health Services Administration (2016) *Impact of the DSM-IV to DSM-5 Changes on the National Survey on Drug Use and Health*. Rockville, MD: Substance Abuse and Mental Health Services Administration (US), June, Table 3.15, DSM-IV to DSM-5 Generalized Anxiety Disorder Comparison. www.ncbi.nlm.nih.gov/books/NBK519704/table/ch3.t15/

Symonds, J. E. and Galton, M. (2014) Moving to the next school at age 10–14 years: an international review of psychological development at school transition. *Review of Education*, 2(1), pp. 1–27.

Taylor, K. and Trott, M. (1996) Pyramid of learning. In M. S Williams and S. Shellenberger (eds), *How Does Your Engine Run: A Leader's Guide to the Alert Program for Self-Regulation*. London: Therapy Works, pp. 1–5.

Temirpulotovich, T. B. (2023) Effects of social factors in children with anxiety-phobic disorders. *Journal of Healthcare and Life-Science Research*, 2(10), pp. 35–41. https://jhlsr.innovascience.uz/index.php/jhlsr/article/view/238

The Makaton Charity (2022) *About Makaton*. www.makaton.org/TMC/AboutMakaton.aspx?hkey=c8a4263d-78cc-4c30-b135-153eb6ac3118

The National Archives (1998) The Human Rights Act. www.legislation.gov.uk/ukpga/1998/42/contents

Thich Nhat Hanh (2017) *The Art of Living: mindful techniques for peaceful living from one of the world's most revered spiritual leaders*. London: Rider.

Toivo, R. (2023) Authority and agency. In L. Underwood (ed.), *Cultural History of Youth in the Renaissance*. London: Bloomsbury Academic, pp 147–66, 210, 214–53.

United Nations (UN) (2022) *COVID-19: Education Risks Becoming 'Greatest Divider'*. https://news.un.org/en/story/2022/03/1114932

Vinales, J. J. (2013) Evaluation of Makaton in practice by children's nursing students. *Nursing Children and Young People*, 25(3), pp. 14–17. doi: 10.7748/ncyp2013.04.25.3.14.e153. PMID: 23691900

Walker, M. (1987) *The Makaton Vocabulary: Uses and Effectiveness*. https://eric.ed.gov/?id=ED291193

Wang, R. (2021) The influence of attachment types on academic performance of children. *Proceedings of the 2021 4th International Conference on Humanities Education and Social Sciences*. www.atlantis-press.com/proceedings/ichess-21/125966960

Wang, Y., Douglass, S. and Yip, T. (2017) Longitudinal relations between ethnic/racial identity process and content: exploration, commitment, and salience among diverse adolescents. *Developmental Psychology*, 53(11), pp. 2154–69.

Ward, B. and associates (1995) *Good Grief: Exploring Feelings, Loss and Death With Under Elevens. A Holistic Approach*. 2nd edn. London: Jessica Kingsley.

Warnock, H. M. (1978) *Special Educational Needs: Report of the Committee of Enquiry into the Education of Handicapped Children and Young People*. The Warnock Report. London: HMSO.

Waters, E. and Cummings, E. M. (2000) A secure base from which to explore close relationships. *Child Development*, 71(1), pp. 164–72. https://doi.org/10.1111/1467-8624.00130

Waters, H. S. and Waters, E. (2006) The attachment working models concept: among other things, we build script-like representations of secure base experiences. *Attachment and Human Development*, 8(3), pp. 185–97. https://doi.org/10.1080/14616730600856016

Watson, K. (2005) *Hearing the Voice of Gifted and Talented Pupils Through the Use of Learning Logs in Order to Improve Teaching Provision*. London: NAGTY.

Webber, C., Santi, E., Cebula, K., Crompton, C. J. and McGeown, S. (2024) Representation of neurodivergence in fiction books: exploring neurodivergent young peoples' perspectives. *Literacy*. https://psycnet.apa.org/record/2024-80903-001

Weis, M., Trommsdorff, G. and Muñoz, L. (2016) Children's self-regulation and school achievement in cultural contexts: the role of maternal restrictive control. *Frontiers in Psychology*, 7, p. 722.

Widen, S. C. and Russell, J. A. (2008) Young children's understanding of other's emotions. *Handbook of Emotions*, 3, pp. 348–63.

Williford, A. P., Carter, L. M. and Pianta, R. C. (2016) Attachment and school readiness. In J. Cassidy and P. R. Shaver (eds), *Handbook of Attachment: Theory, Research, and Clinical Applications*. 3rd edn. New York: Guilford Press, pp. 966–82.

Wong, C. (2024) Measles outbreaks cause alarm: what the data say. *Nature*. www.nature.com/articles/d41586-024-00265-8

Wong, S. C. Y. and Shum, K. K. M. (2024) Exploring similarities and differences between shyness and social anxiety: an analysis of their relations with social emotional and language outcomes in Hong Kong kindergarteners. *International Journal of Early Childhood*, June, pp. 1–22.

World Health Organization (WHO) (2022) *Constitution*. www.who.int/about/governance/constitution

Wright, B., Tindall, L., Scott, A. J., Lee, E., Cooper, C., Biggs, K., Bee, P., Wang, H. I., Gega, L., Hayward, E. and Solaiman, K. (2023) One session treatment (OST) is equivalent to multi-session cognitive behavioral therapy (CBT) in children with specific phobias (ASPECT): results from a national non-inferiority randomized controlled trial. *Journal of Child Psychology and Psychiatry*, 64(1), pp. 39–49. https://acamh.onlinelibrary.wiley.com/doi/full/10.1111/jcpp.13665

Young Minds (2024) *Depression*. www.youngminds.org.uk/young-person/mental-health-conditions/depression/

Zeanah, C. H., Berlin, L. J. and Boris, N. W. (2011) Practitioner review: clinical applications of attachment theory and research for infants and young children. *Journal of Child Psychology and Psychiatry*, 52(8), pp. 819–33. https://doi.org/10.1111/j.1469-7610.2011.02399.x

INDEX

Zeitfracht Medien GmbH
Ferdinand-Jühlke-Straße 7
99095 Erfurt, Deutschland
produktsicherheit@kolibri360.de